7.50

John Gay:

An Annotated Checklist of Criticism

John Gay:

An Annotated Checklist of Criticism

by

Julie Thompson Klein

The Whitston Publishing Company
Troy, New York
1974

152690

012
G-285k

For
Christof Wegelin
And
Donald S. Taylor

PREFACE

G. B. Underhill summarized the popular critical dismissal from which John Gay suffered for too many years in the "Introductory Memoir" to his 1893 edition of Gay's works:

> The complete lack of independence which forms so distinguishing a feature of the character of John Gay must strike the most superficial reader of his life. He seems to have begun his career under the impression that it was somebody's duty to provide for him in the world; and this impression clung to him through nearly the whole of a lifetime. [1]

Unfortunately, it clung to him longer than his own lifetime and, coupled with Dr. Johnson's judgment of him as a poet "of a lower order," a remark which Johnson originally overheard, this assessment clearly inhibited more readers than encouraged them. Yet such evaluations are hardly the standard of twentieth-century criticism which, led by the work of Sven M. Armens, Bertrand Bronson and many others, has recognized the depth and extent of Gay's satiric thrust. Armens himself noted the central dilemma of scholarship on Gay in his 1954 study:

> Even the most competent critics of Gay have yielded somewhat to the notion that Gay's real excellence lies only in his songs and descriptive powers with the concomitant implication that he was keen in his wit but

[1] John Underhill, "Introductory Memoir," *Poems of John Gay* (London: George Routledge and Sons, 1893), pp. lxiii-lxiv.

superficial. [2]

Armens' book-length investigation of Gay's works encouraged our serious appreciation of Gay and has been supplemented amply by work in periodicals, books and dissertations. Hence, an annotated checklist of this criticism has become a necessary tool. In this volume I have attempted to assemble the relevant materials for both student and scholar; overall I have annotated eighteenth and nineteenth-century studies and as many twentieth-century works as possible. Of course, no checklist can be complete and I do welcome and encourage additions and corrections.

If I have not examined a work myself, I have placed an asterisk by the item; generally that item is sufficiently difficult to obtain that it is only available in selected research libraries in the United States or in foreign libraries. This checklist will be most useful if the following guidelines are observed:

I *Selected Primary Materials.* Since it is not my purpose to survey editions, I have indicated the major editions only.

II *Annotated Secondary Materials*

A. Biographical Reviews and Essays. Early reviewers of Gay often pieced together a short sketch with random comments on works; so, I have placed items which are predominantly biographical here. Those which concentrate more on his works than on his life can be found in either C or L.

B. Letters. Only items referring to the location and nature of Gay's letter writing are here; articles which use letters in discussions of individual works are included in sections on those works.

C. General and Miscellaneous Reviews and Essays. General discussions of Gay's works are here with an indication of the item's major emphasis. The general, book-length studies of Gay are located in this section.

D. *Rural Sports*

---

[2] Sven M. Armens, *John Gay, Social Critic* (New York: King's Crown Press, 1954), p. 224.

E. *The Shepherd's Week*

F. *Trivia*

G. *The Fables*

H. Other Poetical Works.   These items concentrate on specific minor works; general discussions which include references to individual poems are in C.

I. *The Beggar's Opera*.   These items concentrate primarily on *The Beggar's Opera*, though some do include references to *Polly* and other dramas.

J. Productions of *The Beggar's Opera*.

K. *Polly*.   Reviews of productions of *Polly* are interfiled in alphabetical order with discussions of *Polly*.

L. Other Dramatic Works and General Essays on Drama.

M. Dissertations and Theses.

Finally, I wish to thank the many people who have assisted me with this project.   The "List of Bibliographical Sources" indicates all of the bibliographical tools which I have used.   For the use of their combined research facilities, I thank once more the staffs of the University of Michigan libraries.   The project itself has been advanced through the generous support of the Wayne State University Grant-in-Aid program, which enabled me to obtain the assistance of three capable researchers: Candace L. Bucheit, Richard Lutes, and Jerome Cebelak.

Julie Thompson Klein

Detroit, Michigan
July 1972

LIST OF BIBLIOGRAPHICAL SOURCES

1 *Abstracts of English Studies.* Boulder, Colorado, 1 (1958)-15 (1971).

2 Arnott, James Fullerton and John William Robinson. *English Theatrical Literature, 1559-1900: a bibliography incorporating Robert W. Lowe's A bibliographical account of English theatrical literature published in 1888.* London: The Society for Theatre Research, 1970.

3 *Bibliographic Index: A Cumulative Bibliography of Bibliographies.* New York: H. W. Wilson, 1 (1937)-10 (1970).

4 *Biography Index: A Cumulative Index to Biographical Material in Books and Magazines.* New York: H. W. Wilson, 1 (January 1946)-26 (May 1972).

5 *The Book Review Digest.* New York: H. W. Wilson, 1 (1905)-67 (1971).

6 *Book Review Index.* Detroit: Gale Research Company, 1 (1965)-4 (1968).

7 *British Humanities Index* (formerly *Subject Index to Periodicals*). London: Library Association, 1915-1971.

8 *The British National Bibliography Annual.* London: The Council of The British National Bibliography, British Museum, 1950-1970.

9   (*The New*) *Cambridge Bibliography of English Literature.*
    Ed. George Watson. Cambridge: The University Press,
    1971. II (1660-1800), 497-500.

10 Coleman, Arthur and Gary R. Tyler. *Drama Criticism. Vol-
    ume One: A Checklist of Interpretation Since 1940 of Eng-
    lish and American Plays.* Denver: Alan Swallow, 1960.

11 *Cumulative Book Index.* New York: H. W. Wilson, 1889/99-
    1971.

12 *Cumulative Dramatic Index, 1909-1949: A Cumulation of the
    F. W. Faxon Co.'s Dramatic Index.* Ed. Frederick Faxon
    (1909-1935), Mary E. Bates (1936-1944), Anne C. Sutherland
    (1942-1949). Boston, Massachusetts: G. K. Hall, 1965.

13 *Dissertation Abstracts: Abstracts of Dissertations and Mono-
    graphs in microform.* Ann Arbor: University Microfilms,
    1 (1938)-32 (1972).
    Issued as *Microfilm Abstracts* from 1 (1938)-11 (1951).

14 *Dissertations in English and American Literature: Theses
    Accepted by American, British, and German Universities
    1865-1964.* Ed. Lawrence F. McNamee. New York: Bowker,
    1968.

15 *Doctoral Dissertations Accepted by American Universities.*
    New York: H. W. Wilson, 1 (1933/34)-22 (1954/55).
    After 1955 this bibliography continues in the thirteenth
    issue of *Dissertation Abstracts* with the title *Index to
    American Doctoral Dissertations* and is then published
    by University Microfilms. After 1963 the title is *Ameri-
    can Doctoral Dissertations.* (1955/56-1971).

16 *Essay and General Literature Index.* New York: H. W. Wilson,
    1900-1971.

17 Forsgren, Adina. "Bibliography." *John Gay, Poet "of a
    Lower Order": or, Comments on His Rural Poems and Other
    Rural Writings.* Stockholm: Natur Och Kultur, 1964, pp.
    212-214.

18 *An Index to Book Reviews in The Humanities.* Detroit, 1 (1960)-11 (1970).

19 *Master Abstracts: abstracts of selected masters theses on microfilm.* Ann Arbor: University Microfilms, 1962-1972.

20 *Modern Humanities Research Association: Annual Bibliography of English Language and Literature.* Cambridge: Bowes and Bowes, 1920-1971.

21 *Modern Language Association International Bibliography.* New York: MLA, 1921-1971.

22 ["Bibliography" in] *The Ninth Music Book, Containing John Gay and the Ballad Opera (The Beggar's Opera).* London: Hinrichsen, 1956, pp. 50-55.

23 *Oxford Bibliographical Society: Bibliography in Britain.* Oxford: Oxford Bibliographical Society, 1 (1962)-5 (1966).

24 Annual Bibliography *Philological Quarterly*, 5 (1926)-49 (1972). Bibliographies for 1926-1960 collected in *English Literature 1660-1800: A Bibliography of Modern Studies Compiled for Philological Quarterly.* Princeton: Princeton University Press, 1 (1926-1938)-4 (1957-1960).

25 *Poetry Explication; A Checklist of Interpretation Since 1925 of British and American Poems, Past and Present.* Rev. ed. Denver: Swallow, 1962.

26 *Poole's Index to Periodical Literature, 1802-1907.* New York: Peter Smith, 1938.

27 *Reader's Guide to Periodical Literature.* New York: H. W. Wilson, 1 (1901)-72 (1972).
   Before 1900: *Nineteenth Century Reader's Guide to Periodical Literature 1890-1899, with Supplementary Indexing 1900-1922.* Ed. Helen Cushing and Adah Morris. New York: H. W. Wilson, 1944.

28 *A Register of Eighteenth Century Bibliographies and References, A Chronological Quarter-Century Survey.* Ed.

Francesco Cordasco. Chicago: V. Giorgio, 1950; rpt. Detroit: Gale Research, 1969.

29 *Restoration and Eighteenth-Century Theatre Research.* Chicago: Loyola, 1 (1962)-9 (1970).
   Before 1963 title is *Seventeenth and Eighteenth-Century Theatre Research.*

30 *Restoration and Eighteenth-Century Theatre Research: A Bibliographical Guide, 1900-1968.* Ed. Carl J. Stratman, et.al. Carbondale and Edwardsville: Southern Illinois University Press, 1971, pp. 323-338.

31 Schultz, William Eben. "Bibliography." *Gay's Beggar's Opera; Its Content, History and Influence.* New Haven: Yale University Press, 1923, pp. 378-384.

32 *A Selective Index to Theatre Magazine* by Stan Cornyn. New York and London: The Scarecrow Press, 1964.

33 *Social Sciences and Humanities Index* (formerly *International Index to Periodicals*). New York: H. W. Wilson, 1 (1907)-59 (1972).

34 Spacks, Patricia. "Selected Bibliography." *John Gay.* New York: Twayne, 1965, pp. 172-174.

35 *Studies in Bibliography: Papers of the Bibliographical Society of the University of Virginia.* Charlottesville, Virginia: Bibliographical Society of the University of Virginia, 1 (1948-49)-21 (1968).
   The first three volumes run under the title *Papers of the Bibliographical Society of the University of Virginia.*

36 Tobin, James Edward. *Eighteenth-Century English Literature and Its Cultural Background.* New York: Fordham University Press, 1939.

37 *The Year's Work in English Studies.* London: Oxford University Press, 1 (1919-20)-50 (1969). Edited for The English Association (London).

CHRONOLOGY

1685 Born in Barnstaple (June 30)

       Baptized at Barnstaple Old Church (September 16)

1695 Approximate date of attendance at Barnstaple Grammar School

1702 Approximate date of arrival in London to be apprentice to silk mercer

1706 Quits apprenticeship and returns briefly to Barnstaple

1707 (Approx.) Returns to London and becomes secretary to Aaron Hill

1708 *Wine* published (May)

1709 Verses *To the Learned Ingenious Author of Licentia Poetica Discuss'd* appear

1711 *The Present State of Wit* published (May 3)

1712 Becomes secretary to the Duchess of Monmouth *The Mohocks* published (April 15)

       An Argument proving that the present Mohocks and Hawkubites are the Gog and Magog mention'd in the Revelation published anonymously.

       Epistle to Lintott and *The Story of Arachne* appear in Lintott's Miscellany (May)

1713   *Rural Sports* published (January 13)

      Authors papers in *The Guardian: Reproof and Flattery* (March 24) and *Dress* (September 21)

      The Wife of Bath produced at Drury Lane Theatre (May 12)

      The Fan published (December 8)

      Panthea, Araminta, A Thought on Eternity and *A Contemplation on Night* appear in Steele's *Poetical Miscellany* (December 29)

1714   *The Shepherd's Week* published (April 15)

      Appointed secretary to Lord Clarendon (June 8); accompanies Clarendon to Hanover (June through September)

      Appointment terminates on death of Queen Anne (August 1)

      A Letter to a Lady published (November 20)

1715   *The What d'ye Call It* produced at Drury Lane (February 23)

      The What d'ye Call It published (March 19)

      Visits Exeter at Lord Burlington's expense (summer)

      Writes *Epistle to Burlington*

1716   *Trivia* published (January 26)

      Court Poems (including *The Toilette*) published (March 26)

      Visits Devonshire again; then journeys to Bath (July)

1717   *Three Hours After Marriage* produced at Drury Lane (January 16)

      Three Hours After Marriage published (January 21)

      Visits Continent with Pulteneys

Responsible for most of Ninth Book of Ovid's *Metamor-phoses*, edited by Garth.

Horace, Epod.iv. Imitated by James Baker Kt. appears under pseud. (approximately July)

Letter to W--L--, Esq. published (Autumn)

Epistle to Pulteney published

1718 Visits Cockthorpe and Stanton Harcourt, seats of Lord Harcourt in Oxfordshire

1719 Second visit to the Continent

1720 *Poems on Several Occasions* published and results in large profit

Loses profit in South Sea Bubble (stock crisis)

Daphnis and Cloe. A New Song appears with music

Sweet William's Farewell to Black-ey'd Susan appears with music

Mr. Pope's Welcome from Greece written

1721 *A Panegyrical Epistle to Mr. Thomas Snow* published (February 8)

Visits Bath

Frequent association with Lord Burlington and the Duchess of Queensberry

1722 *Epistle to Her Grace, Henrietta, Duchess of Marlborough* published (July 11)

1723 Appointed Lottery Commissioner

Spends summer with Burlingtons at Tunbridge Wells

Reads *The Captives* to the Princess of Wales

1724   *The Captives* produced at Drury Lane (January 15)

The Captives published

A Poem Address'd to the Quidnunc's appears anonymously

Spends time in Lord Burlington's household

Spends holiday at Bath with Dr. Arbuthnot

1725   *To a Lady on Her Passion for Old China, Newgate's Garland* published

Begins work on *Fables* and seeks court preferment

Blueskin's Ballad appears anonymously (1724-25)

Newgate's Ballad appears anonymously

1726   *Molly Mog* appears in Mist's Journal (August 27) and then in broadside with music, anonymously

1727   *The Fables* (V. I) published

Declines post of Gentleman-Usher to Princess Louisa (October)

Several poems of possible authorship appear in Pope-Swift miscellany; including *Nelly, Ballad on Quadrille, New Song of New Similes,* and *Ay and No.*

The Coquet Mother and Coquet Daughter appear in Richard Steele miscellany (possible authorship)

1728   *The Beggar's Opera* produced at Lincoln's Inn Fields (January 29)

The Beggar's Opera published (February 14)

Polly prohibited (December 12)

1729 *Polly* published (approximately March)

Loses lodgings in Whitehall; then lives with Queensberrys

The Banished Beauty; or a Fair Face in Disgrace appears anonymously

1730 *The Wife of Bath* produced unsuccessfully at Lincoln's Inn Fields (January 19)

1731 Relinquishes post of Lottery Commissioner

1732 *Acis and Galatea* produced at Haymarket (May)

Finishes second volume of *Fables*

Visits Sir William Wyndham at Orchard Wyndham (September through October)

Verses to be Placed under the Picture of England's Arch-Poet and *An Epitaph of Big Words* appear in Motte and Gulliver *Miscellanies* (possible authorship)

Dies (December 3)

Buried in Westminster Abbey (December 23)

1733 *Achilles* produced at Lincoln's Inn Fields (February 10)

1734 *The Distress'd Wife* produced

1738 V. II of *The Fables* published

1743 *The Distress'd Wife* published

1754 *The Rehearsal at Goatham* published

1777 *Polly* first produced

1820 *Gay's Chair: Poems Never Before Printed* published

1910 *Some Unpublished Translations from Ariosto* published

TABLE OF CONTENTS

I

SELECTED PRIMARY MATERIALS

Vinton Dearing is now preparing a definitive edition of the poems for the Oxford English Texts series of Clarendon Press; in the meantime, the standard edition of Gay's works, which includes several plays and all of the poems, is *The Poetical Works of John Gay.* Ed. G. C. Faber. Oxford: The University Press, 1926. Faber's edition may be supplemented by the following:

Gay, John. *The Beggar's Opera, A Faithful Reproduction of the 1729 Edition.* Larchmont, New York: Argonaut Books, 1961. Includes words of adapted tunes.

---. *Gay's Chair, Poems Never Before Printed.* Ed. Joseph Baller, 1820.

---. *The Plays of John Gay.* London: Chapman and Dodd, 1923. The Abbey Classics, XIV and XV.

---. *The Present State of Wit* (1711). Ed. Donald F. Bond. Los Angeles: Clark Library, 1947. Augustan Reprint Society Publication No. 7.

---. *Some Unpublished Translations from Ariosto.* Ed. J. D. Bruce. Brunswick, 1910.

---, Alexander Pope and John Arbuthnot. *Three Hours After Marriage.* Ed. Richard Morton and William Peterson. Painesville, Ohio: Lake Erie College Studies, 1961.

John Gay

---. *Three Hours After Marriage.* Ed. John Harrington Smith.
  Los Angeles: Clark Library, 1961. Augustan Reprint Society
  Publications 91 and 92.

ANNOTATED CHECKLIST

Biographical Reviews and Essays

A1 "An Account of the Life and Writings of the Author." *Plays
Written by Mr. John Gay, viz. a Tragedy. The Beggar's
Opera, Polly, or the Second Part of The Beggar's Opera,
Achilles, an Opera, The Distress'd Wife, a comedy, The
Rehearsal at Goatham, a Farce. To which is added, An
Account of the Life and Writings of the Author.* London:
Printed For J. & R. Tonson, 1760, pp. iii-xii.
Review of career with previously unprinted verse,
fable by Gay and Pope's long inscription for him.

A2 *Biographica Britannica: Or, the Lives of the Most Eminent
Persons who have Flourished in Great Britain and Ireland.*
London: Printed for W. Meadows, et.al., 1757, pp. 2182-
2188.
Review of career with copious notes on background
of works, using letters, journals and contemporary
reactions to *Shepherd's Week, What d'ye Call It* and
Three Hours After Marriage.

A3 Blackwell, Alfred E. "John Gay (1685-1732)." *The Devonshire Association for the Advancement of Science, Literature and Art,* 87 (1955), 116-129.
Review of career with illustrations, including history
and description of Gay's chair; gives *Trivia* high
praise.

A4 *British Authors Before 1880.* Ed. Stanley Kunitz and Howard
 Haycraft. New York: Wilson, 1952, pp. 212-214 with
 portrait.
 Review of standard information: Gay lazy, idle and
 amiable.

A5 *Chamber's Cyclopaedia of English Literature.* Ed. David
 Patrick. Philadelphia and New York: J. B. Lippincott,
 1901. II, 172-178.
 Study of Gay's political foibles with numerous quotes
 from works: *Trivia, Fables* (his best) and several
 ballads.

A6 Cibber, Theopilus. "Mr. Gay." *The Lives of the Poets of
 Great Britain and Ireland.* London: Printed for R. Griffiths,
 1753. IV, 250-259.
 Biography with Pope's letter welcoming Gay, notes on
 success of *Beggar's Opera,* part of Swift's vindication
 of *Beggar's Opera,* Gay's account of *Polly's* trouble,
 sketchy review of plays, and Pope's epitaph. Gay
 amiable, indolent; pastorals have "highest finishing"
 of works.

A7 Curll, Edmund. *The Life of Mr. John Gay, Author of The
 Beggar's Opera.* London: Printed for E. Curll, 1733.
 Biographical review with generous quotes from works.
 Curll reprints letter examining *What d'ye Call It,*
 and concludes Gay's Horatian-like epistles superior
 to Boileau's.

A8 *Dictionary of National Biography.* Ed. Leslie Stephen. London: Smith, Elder and Co., 1890. XXII, 83-90.
 Biographical review with emphasis on friendships
 and Gay's eclogues and songs. *Trivia* "a mine of
 not-yet-overworked information respecting the details
 of outdoor life under Anne."

A9 Gay, John. *Fables by John Gay, with a Life of the Author
 and Embellished with Seventy Plates.* London: Printed
 for John Stockdale, 1793. I, 163-175.
 Biographical and career review.

A10 Gaye, Phoebe. *John Gay, His Place in the Eighteenth Century.* London: Collins, 1938.

> Biographical review which is inferior to Irving book: lacks research notes and tends to speculation and metaphor, which interferes with factual data. Gaye emphasizes background of works and friends, with frequent use of letters.
> Rev. by Ifor Evans in *Fortnightly Review,* 150 (October 1938), 493.
> Rev. in *Times Literary Supplement,* 17 September 1938, p. 601.

A11 Irving, William Henry. *John Gay, Favorite of the Wits.* Durham, N.C.: Duke University Press, 1940.

> Best biography with careful research notes, use of letters and in-depth factual study, though background is often developed in surplus. *Shepherd's Week* began as burlesque of Virgil, not ridicule of Philips. *Yarhell's Kitchen* by Gay, not Prior as Faber says; also considers several other disputed authorships. Pope encouraged *What d'ye Call It;* it was a frequent response for help on Gay's part. Irving carefully considers contemporary reactions to works, including years of pre-*Beggar's Opera* suggestions.
> Rev. in *Books,* 1 September 1940, p. 11.
> Rev. by John Butt in *Review of English Studies,* 17 (April 1941), 226-227.
> Rev. by Charles K. Eves in *Modern Language Notes,* 57 (April 1942), 300-311.
> Rev. by W. H. Irving in *Times Literary Supplement,* 31 August 1940, p. 427.
> Rev. in *Nation,* 7 September 1940, p. 199.
> Rev. in *New Republic,* 20 May 1940, p. 681.
> Rev. in *New York Times,* 19 May 1940, p. 24.
> Rev. in *South West Review,* 26 (1940), 265-267.
> Rev. in *Spectator,* 5 July 1940, p. 22.
> Rev. in *Theatre Arts,* 24 (August 40), 614.

A12 "John Gay." *Supplement to the Universal Magazine,* 35 (December 1764), 337-345.

> Memoir of sweet and simple Gay, whose purse was a barometer of his spirits: includes discussion of

> *What d'ye Call It, Polly*, Gay's improper epitaph.
> His pastorals, though allied to Pope, were successful;
> however, they were not a true copy of the country.

A13 Johnson, Samuel. *Lives of the English Poets*. Ed. George
Birbeck Hill. Oxford: Clarendon Press, 1905, pp. 267-
285.

> Gay a light spirit, not real "partner" of the wits.
> His pastorals were popular; *Beggar's Opera* ridiculed
> Italian drama, but only for diversion, not for moral
> purpose since Macheath is reprieved. In all, Gay was
> a poet "of a lower order" who lacked true poetic
> genius.

A14 Kearley-Wright, W. H. *John Gay, Biography*. London: Frederick Warne, 1923, pp. 11-51.

> Edition of *Fables* with bibliography of other editions
> and thorough essay on Gay's life which emphasizes
> political fortunes and corrects birthdate from 1688 to
> 1685. *Shepherd's Week*, marred by "Proeme," incited
> by Pope and printed at Bolingbroke's desire. Pope
> and Swift assisted with *Beggar's Opera*. Final praise
> goes for ballads, proverbs and attempts at various
> genres, though Kearley-Wright displays ambiguous mix-
> ture of pity and condemnation for Gay's failures.

A15 *Cyclopedia of World Authors*. Ed. Frank N. Magill. New
York: Harper, 1958, pp. 409-411.

> Brief: only contains standard information.

A16 Melville, Lewis (pseud. for Lewis S. Benjamin). *Life and
Letters of John Gay (1685-1732) Author of "The Beggar's
Opera."* London: Daniel O'Connor, 1921; rpt. Folcraft,
Pa.: Folcroft Press, 1969.

> Biographical review which strives for sense of im-
> mediate reaction of Gay's friends with narrative use
> of letters. *Shepherd's Week* written for Pope, yet
> independently successful; *Three Hours* a "sorry
> piece," and *Beggar's Opera* has charms but not a
> great literary piece. After 1723, Melville relies
> greatly on letters, particularly final correspondence
> with Pope and Swift. Appendices include H. W. G.

Flood's short notes on sources of *Beggar's Opera*
tunes, chronological list of 120 letters (to and from),
and program of 1920 Hammersmith revival.
Rev. in *Bookman* (London), 61 (October 1921), 33-34.
Rev. in *Times Literary Supplement*, 22 September
1921, p. 608.

A17 Owen, Octavius Freire. "Life of John Gay." *The Fables
of John Gay Illustrated, with an original memoir, introduction and annotations.* London: George Routledge,
1854, pp. 1-9.
Review of career marked by tendency towards "con-
tented servility," "fickleness of fortune" and independence.

A18 Ruhe, E. L. "Pope's Hand in Thomas Birch's Account of
Gay." *Review of English Studies*, n.s. 5 (April 1954),
171-174.
Thomas Birch's biography of Gay (1736) contained
previously unpublished Pope letter to Savage regarding Gay's family and position.

A19 Sherwin, Oscar. *Mr. Gay, Being a Picture of the Life and
Times of the Author of the Beggar's Opera.* New York:
John Day, 1929.
Inferior to Irving biography: reviews life with present-
tense narrative and simple style. *Shepherd's Week*
written in support of Pope, though Gay did become
immersed in his rural interests. Rhapsodically, Sher-
win builds portrait of Gay's financial and political
fortunes, Lavinia Fenton and success of *Beggar's
Opera*, using Swift and Gay's correspondence. Wal-
pole responsible for *Polly's* troubles.
Rev. by Vera Kelsey in *Theatre Arts Monthly*, 13
(October 1929), 788.
Rev. in *Theatre*, 50 (August 1929), 4.
Rev. by F. T. Wood in sketch in *Bookman* (London),
83 (October 1932), 162-164.

A20 Untermeyer, Louis. *Lives of the Poets.* New York: Simon
and Schuster, 1959, pp. 220-221.

Brief review: Gay authored "satire without spite."

A21 Warner, Oliver. *Writers and Their Works.* London: Longmans, Green and Co., 1964.

Review with generous quotes. *Shepherd's Week* partly satirized Philips, mocks older pastoral style. Pre-*Beggar's Opera* dramas not too successful; songs and ballad opera quite good. Reviews of *Beggar's Opera* and *Polly* are extensive but the bibliography is skimpy.

Letters

B1 Burgess, C. F. "The John Gay of the Letters." *The Letters of John Gay.* Oxford: Clarendon Press, 1966, pp. xv-xxiii. Assessment of characters reflected in letters.

B2 ---. "John Gay to the Countess of Burlington: An Unpublished Letter." *Philological Quarterly,* 43 (July 1964), 420-422. Gay's chatty letter (28 August 1726) to Burlingtons on 1726 tour of Continent more carefully written than ordinarily less kempt style for Pope and Swift: includes account of seeing Settle's *Siege of Troy* and *Bartholomew Fair.*

B3 ---. "A Missing Gay Letter Located." *Notes and Queries,* 260 (1964), 56-57. Gay letter (27 June 1714) to Charles Ford (previously in Swift collection) written in Gay's typical epistolary style: "Witty," "Charming" and concerned with trivia.

B4 Melville, Lewis (pseud, for Lewis S. Benjamin). *Life and Letters of John Gay (1685-1732) Author of "The Beggar's Opera."* London: Daniel O'Connor, 1921; rpt. Folcraft, Pa.: Folcraft Press, 1969. Narrative presentation of letters in biography format.

B5 Passon, Richard H. "Gay to Swift on Political Satire." *American Notes and Queries,* 3 (February 1965), 87. Gay's letter (16 Aug. 1714) to Swift about King of France's Academy to teach politics as a science may have inspired Gulliver's deploration of Brobdingnag's failure to reduce politics to a science (*Gulliver's Travels,* Bk. 2, Ch. 7).

B6 Rawson, C. J. "Some Unpublished Letters of Pope and Gay, and Some Manuscript Sources of Goldsmith's *Life of Thomas Parnell.*" *Review of English Studies*, n.s. 10 (November 1959), 371-387.

> Gay's letters in ms. collection of Parnell family concern activities of Scriblerus Club, including Parnell's health and affairs.

B7 Sherburn, George. "Gibberish in 1730-1." *Notes and Queries*, 198 (April 1953), 160-161.

> Reprint of letter from Viscount Percival to son contains gibberish which Duchess of Queensberry used; Swift played language games in correspondence with Queensberrys and Gay.

B8 Tickell, Richard Eustace. *Thomas Tickell and the Eighteenth Century Poets (1685-1740).* London: Constable, 1931, pp. 77 and 131.

> Includes undated letter of thanks for subscription from Gay and comment in letter (5 June 1727) to Young that only about five of Gay's *Fables* tolerable.

General and Miscellaneous Reviews and Essays

C1 Aitken, George A. "John Gay." *The Westminster Review,*
140 (October 1893), 386-403.
Review of life and troubles with politics, finances
and general indolence. *Shepherd's Week* written at
Pope's request; best work was songs, though reputation rests on *Beggar's Opera* and *Fables.*

C2 Armens, Sven M. *John Gay, Social Critic.* New York: King's
Crown Press, 1954.
Comprehensive study using town-country contrast and
man-beast affinity as measure of values in Gay's
works. *Rural Sports* reveals ideal values, while *Shepherd's Week* shows incompatability of describing modern British rural matter in strict Virgilian form and
theme of healthy functionalism. Overall, Gay perceives
dichotomy between beast and spirit, between reason
and self-interest. Appendix contains chart of themes in
Fables.
Rev. by Donald F. Bond in *Modern Philology,* 53
(November 1955), 131-134.
Rev. by J. P. Brawner in *South Atlantic Quarterly,*
60 (April 1956), 246-247.
Rev. by Herbert Cahoon in *Library Journal,* 1 December
1954, p. 2314.
Rev. by Hörst Hohne in *Zeitzchrift für Anglistik und
Amerikanistik,* 5 (1957), 212-215.
Rev. by W. H. Irving in *Philological Quarterly,* 34
(July 1955), 289-290.
Rev. by Jean Jacquot in *Études Anglaises,* 11 (July-
September 1958), 257-258.

Rev. by C. H. Peake in *Review of English Studies,*
n.s. 7 (March 1956), 222.
Rev. in *Times Literary Supplement,* 10 June 1955,
p. 314.
Rev. in *U. S. Quarterly Book Review,* 11 (June 1955),
206-207.

C3   Baring-Gould, Sabine. " 'The Beggar's Opera' and Gay's
Chair." *Devonshire Characters and Strange Events.*
London: John Lane, 1926, pp. 10-20.
Brief sketch on family and career with focus on *Beg-*
gar's Opera, Lavinia Fenton's success, history of
Gay's chair and popular sayings.

C4   Melville, Lewis (pseud. for Lewis S. Benjamin). *Lady Suffolk*
and Her Circle.   London: Hutchinson, 1924.
See index for many references in passing to Gay.

C5   Birrell, Augustine. "John Gay." *Essays About Men, Women,*
and Books.   London: Eliot Stock, 1894, pp. 109-120.
General musing. *Beggar's Opera* his greatest achieve-
ment and *Fables* display best poetic endeavor. Also
available in Birrell's *Collected Essays and Addresses*
of the Rt. Hon. Augustine Birrell, 1880-1920. New York:
Scribner's Sons, 1923, pp. 100-106.

C6   Brown, Wallace Cable. "Gay's Mastery of the Heroic Couplet."
Publications of the Modern Language Association, 61
(March 1946), 114-152.
Comparison to Pope reveals many similar devices in
Gay's couplets: selections from *Rural Sports, Trivia,*
and other works examined plus tone of Gay's satire.
Also available as "Gay: Pope's Alter Ego." *Triumph*
of Form, A Study of the Later Masters of the Heroic
Couplet.   Chapel Hill: University of North Carolina
Press, 1948, pp. 45-66.

C7   Burdett, Osbert. "John Gay." *Critical Essays.* New York:
Henry Holt, 1926, pp. 51-60.
Close review of Gay's *Guardian* essays and songs from
Beggar's Opera. Fables will slip in popularity, with

final reputation resting on songs and dialogue.

* C8 C., F. W. "Portraits of John Gay." *Devon and Cornwall Notes and Queries*, 11 (1920-1921), 287.

C9 Collins, A. S. "Patronage in the Days of Johnson." *Nineteenth Century and After*, 100 (October 1926), 616-617.
Gay born to "recline in the lap of luxury which patronage still fortunately spread out." Though unsuccessful at court, social patrons Burlington, Lincoln and Queensberry supported him.

C10 Colville, Kenneth Newton. "John Gay." *Fame's Twilight: Studies of Nine Men of Letters.* London: P. Allen, 1923, pp. 213-235.
Brief biographical review, discussion of *Achilles, Polly, What d'ye Call It* and morality of *Beggar's Opera.* Reputation first rested on *Fables,* then pastorals, not *Beggar's Opera;* real talent is balladry.

C11 "Common-Place Notes." *The Gentleman's Magazine*, 57 (January 1787), 76.
Gay paid for helping Pope with his Shakespeare ed.

C12 "Curiosities of Brockley Hall." *The Illustrated London News*, 27 October 1849, p. 284.
History of Gay's chair, among auction items.

C13 Dobrée, Bonamy. *English Literature in the Early Eighteenth Century, 1700-1740.* Oxford: Clarendon Press, 1959, pp. 177-182.
Depicts Gay as parasitic type incapable of rivaling Prior, with emphasis on light and "down to earth" qualities. *Fables* his most important contribution.

C14 Dobson, Austin. "John Gay." *Miscellanies.* New York: Dodd, Mead, 1898, pp. 239-274.
Biographical review with emphasis on Gay's indolence and close relationship between his works and friendships; includes background of *Present State of Wit.* Gay's works lack "high philosophical wisdom,"

but show good sense, humor, and practical view of life.

* C15 Eschenburg, von Johan Joachim. *Beispielsanamlung zur Theorie und Literatur der Schönen Wissenschaften.* Berlin und Stettin, 1788.

Reprints verses with discussion of *Beggar's Opera, Polly,* and *Achilles* (Mentioned in Irving, *John Gay,* p. 89).

C16 Fairchild, Hoxie Neal. "Beginnings of Sentimentalism." *Religious Trends in English Poetry.* New York: Columbia University Press, 1939. I, 227-231.

Gay's realism, love for country, interest in Spenser, and fondness for popular sentimentalism anticipate Romanticism; sentimentalism softens his aristocratic bent.

C17 Forsgren, Adina. *John Gay, Poet "of a Lower Order": or, Comments on His Rural Poems and Other Writings.* Stockholm: Natur Och Kultur, 1964.

Exhaustive background study of early works with copious footnotes. Gay preferred "low kinds" of literature with a cheerful realism similar to Hogarth. In early works he blends tradition with attacks on heroic scribblers. *Wine* reveals his direction: "laborious art" with serious themes combined with burlesque, anglicized material. *Rural Sports* is a peace poem with georgic features, related to topographic and pastoral genres and older English poetry. *Shepherd's Week* rejuvenates an old genre in comic mode with modern and low pedantry yet traditional eclogue themes, modern and Scriblerian matter, ballads and other low and anglicized items. Rural characters are both traditional and contemporary. Overall, Gay reacted to scriblers by positively furthering "little Taste" which mixed kinds and added modern to traditional.

Rev. by Sven Armens in *Philological Quarterly,* 44 (July 1965), 350-351.

Rev. by John Chalker in *Studia Neophilologica,* 37 (1965), 256-259.

Rev. by B. Dobée in *Review of English Studies*, 18
(February 1967), 106.
Rev. in *Times Literary Supplement*, 25 November
1965, p. 1063.
Rev. by Clarence Tracy in *Modern Language Review*,
63 (January 1968), 198-199.
Volume II: Comments on His Urban and Narrative Poetry
(1971).

C18 Gay, Ernest L. "Errors and Omissions in the Bibliography
of John Gay in *Cambridge History of English Literature*."
Nation, 24 April 1913, p. 413.
Corrects several errors pertaining to editions, spel-
lings and critical omissions.

C19 Grierson, H. J. C. and J. C. Smith. "The Age of Pope and
Other Augustans." *Critical History of English Poetry*.
Oxford: University Press, 1944, pp. 208-230.
Brief study of friends' influence in *Shepherd's Week*,
"Twas when the seas were roaring," *Trivia*, and
Beggar's Opera.

* C20 Harmonicus, Phil. *Coventry Journal, or The Craftsman*, 17
February 1938.
Contains letter of objection to inappropriate epitaph
of Gay; writer thought to be Samuel Johnson.

C21 Henley, William Ernest. "Gay." *Views and Reviews*. London: David Nutt, 1890, pp. 183-187.
Negative review: *Fables* are "merest journalism"
compared to those of LaFontaine. Henley is some-
what enthused about *Beggar's Opera*, but feels only
the songs really touch us.

C22 Humphreys, Arthur Raleigh. *The Augustan World, Life and
Letters in Eighteenth-Century England*. London:
Methuen, 1954, pp. 43-45, 49-50 and scattered references.
Emphasis on Gay's depiction of England: *Rural Sports*
for rural diversion, *Trivia* for London life, *Beggar's
Opera* for low characters equated with statesmen.
Rural Sports and *Contemplation on Night* depict Augus-
tan "inward cheerfulness" regarding Providence.

C23 Irving, William Henry. *John Gay's London, Illustrated From the Poetry of the Time*. Cambridge: Harvard University Press, 1928; rpt. London: Archon Bks., 1968.

> Quotations used to give impression of London life in Queen Anne's time. Gay's works among many others and are discussed in light of contemporary issues and traditional urban depictions. Appendix contains note on early editions of *Trivia*.
> Rev. by W. T. Morgan in *A. H. R.* 35 (1930), 342-344.
> Rev. by Walter Graham in *Journal of English and Germanic Philology*, 28 (October 1929), 573-574.

C24 Kramnick, Isaac. "John Gay--Beggars, Gentry, and Society." *Bolingbroke and His Circle, The Politics of Nostalgia in the Age of Walpole*. Cambridge: Harvard University Press, 1968, pp. 223-230 and references in passing.

> Gay reflects Opposition mind and Augustan humanist's rejection of urban corruption. *Fables, Beggar's Opera* are nostalgic attacks on Walpole. *Rural Sports* with town-country contrast, king in *Polly*, city-country contrast in *Trivia* all reinforce values. *Beggar's Opera* is "central statement" of Opposition argument, showing affect of money on values and fate of gentry and noblemen in a commercial society when upstart ranks threaten old order.

C25 Lawrence, R. A. "A Relic of the Poet Gay." *Notes and Queries*, 16 December 1882, p. 488.

> Reprints December 7 piece from *North Devon Herald* with notice of pew portion removed from Barnstaple church with name of Gay and date 1695 on it; Gay ten years old then.

C26 Leed, Jacob. "Two New Pieces by Johnson in the *Gentleman's Magazine?*" *Modern Philology*, 54 (May 1957), 221-229.

> October 1736 *Gentleman's Magazine* letter signed Pamphilus is by Johnson because of similarity to his "Essay on Epitaphs."

C27 Liebert, Herman W. "Johnson and Gay." *Notes and Queries,*
12 May 1951, pp. 126-127.

> Objects to identification of Johnson as Pamphilus
> in *Gentleman's Magazine* letter; no evidence of his
> contributions before 1738 and style of his essay is
> not like the letter.

C28 Lynch, Kathleen M. *A Congreve Gallery.* Cambridge: Harvard University Press, 1951, pp. 4, 5, 7, 9, 17, 60-61,
64 , 66.

> Contains several references regarding Gay's friend-
> ship with Congreve.

C29 Mack, Maynard. "Gay Augustan." *Yale University Library
Gazette,* 21 (1946), 6-10.

> Concludes most of Gay's writings are "charming
> piecemeal," though *Beggar's Opera* operates under
> more powerful conviction.

C30 Minto, William. *The Literature of the Georgian Era.* New
York: Harper and Brothers, 1895, pp. 53-54.

> Brief tribute to Gay's song powers; pastorals reveal
> touch of insincerity towards rustics because he bur-
> lesques their sentiments.

C31 Nichols, John. *Literary Anecdotes of the Eighteenth Century;
Comprizing Biographical Memoirs of William Bowyer,
Printer.* London: Printed for the Author by Nichols, Son
and Bentley, 1812.

> v, p. 597: Lists price Gay paid for help with Pope's
> Shakespeare edition.
> vi, p. 845: Includes letters about *Rural Sports, Windsor
> Forest,* and *Cato.*
> viii, p. 168: Letter to Congreve re Pope's delay of
> Homer edition.
> p. 296: List of Gay's publications by Lintott with pur-
> chase price.

C32 Paull, H. M. "John Gay." *Fortnightly Review,* 1 June
1912, pp. 1095-1111.

> Reviews life and political foibles, *Polly's* difficul-
> ties, eighteenth and nineteenth-century opinons of

works. Songs are Gay's best contributions; *Fables*
not outstanding; only *Beggar's Opera* will remain
popular. Gay's greatest fault was indolence.

C33 Price, Martin. *To the Palace of Wisdom, Studies in Order
and Energy From Dryden to Blake*. Garden City, New
York: Doubleday, 1964, pp. 245-249, 252-261.
Opposition of avarice and generosity in *Beggar's
Opera* part of Gay's study of conflicting values;
"corruption reduced to artless ease." *Shepherd's
Week* has interplay of formal and loutish jargon which
mocks Philips. *Trivia* mockery is incongruity of classical and contemporary. Gay's mock forms reveal
what people are through study of what they aren't.

C34 Reade, Aleyn Lyell. "Pope's 'Mr. Russel' of 1739." *Notes
and Queries*, 17 June 1939, p. 420.
Picture of Gay in Phoebe Gaye's biography traced
by John Vanderbank; pose and dress similar to style
of William Russel portrait.

C35 Reynolds, Myra. *The Treatment of Nature in English Poetry
Between Pope and Wordsworth*. New York: Gordian,
1967, pp. 64-68 and references to diction.
Catalogues references to hills, flowers and animals,
but ignores irony of *Shepherd's Week*. Gay helped
turn poetry from artificial to natural by showing incongruity of Latin form and natural pastoral.

C36 Saintsbury, G. E. B. *The Peace of the Augustans, A Survey
of Eighteenth-Century Literature As a Place of Rest
and Refreshment*. London: G. Bell, 1916, pp. 58-60.
Gay's touches of brilliance belong to Pope, Swift
and Arbuthnot. Gay himself was of a lower order
and lacks universality.

C37 Seccombe, Thomas. "Lesser Verse Writers." *The Cambridge
History of English Literature*. Ed. Ward and Waller.
New York: G. P. Putnam's, 1913. IX, 179-184.
Review of Gay's career includes *Rural Sports* (smooth
reflection of Pope's own pastoral), *Beggar's Opera*,
Shepherd's Week and *Trivia*. In all, Gay depended

greatly on Swift and Duchess of Queensberry.

C38 Sherburn, George. *The Early Career of Alexander Pope*.
       Oxford: Clarendon Press, 1934, pp. 137-139, 192-198,
       149-151 and references in passing.
          References to Scriblerus Club members; many of
          Gay's works between 1714-1716 show "bias in
          favour of Pope."

C39 ---. "The Restoration and Eighteenth Century (1660-1789)."
       A Literary History of England. Ed. Albert C. Baugh. New
       York: Appleton Century Crofts, 1948, pp. 918-921.
          Career review concludes reputation suffered with
          tales of Pope's assistance, though twentieth century
          recognized Gay's own talents. Informality and bur-
          lesque were his chief traits, though fable *Hare and
          Many Friends* not an autobiographical reproach to
          his friends. Gay was Pope's chief ally in pastoral
          wars and gave much of the country to poetry.

C40 Southey, Robert. *Specimens of the Later English Poets,
       with Preliminary Notices*. London: Printed for
       Longman, Hurst, Rees and Orme, 1807. I, 298.
          Fables most popular of works; eclogues meant to
          ridicule Philips, though Gay's copy of nature and
          "quick and observing eye" showed contemporaries
          a "better taste."

C41 Spacks, Patricia Meyer. *John Gay*. New York: Twayne,
       1965.
          Study of Gay's progress from hiding behind masks
          to manipulating them; contains balance of thesis,
          plot review, standard information and anecdotes,
          plus studies of diction. *Wine* reveals ambivalence
          of burlesque and sincerity. *Rural Sports* closer to
          model, using characteristic method of expansion.
          Shepherd's Week realistic and burlesque with persona
          exposing country values. Point of view shifts between
          serious and trivial in *Trivia,* in which sharp observa-
          tion is Gay's greatest success. Epistles in 1720 col-
          lection show manipulation from innocence to indig-
          nation. *Beggar's Opera* contains complexity of disguises

and levels of imagery; Gay moved from heavy dependence on models to persona of simple man.
Rev. in *Choice*, 3 (March 1966), 35.

C42 Spacks, Patricia Meyer. "John Gay: A Satirist's Progress."
Essays in Criticism, 14 (April 1964), 156-170.
Investigates use of näive pose for satiric purposes
and explores conflict of values between "unwordly
poet" and more business-oriented man; also examines
types of satiric perspectives used in *Fables*, as well
as selected verse epistles and eclogues.

C43 Spence, Joseph. *Anecdotes, Observations and Characters
of Books and Men.* London: Centaur Press, 1964, pp.
39-45, 102-110, 130-196.
(First two editions appeared in 1820). Source of
oft-quoted anecdotes and remarks used by many
critics: includes Gay's role in Scriblerus Club,
Swift's suggestions and Gay's relationship to
friends.

C44 Sutherland, James. "John Gay." *Pope and His Contemporaries: Essays Presented to George Sherburn.* Ed.
James Clifford and Louis Landa. Oxford: Clarendon
Press, 1949, pp. 201-214.
Beggar's Opera, friendship with Pope and Swift,
and Dr. Johnson's judgment still influence Gay's
reputation. On own terms, Gay skilled craftsman
who softens actual with contrast between natural
and artificial. Examples, including "Birth of the
Squire," show his skill in satire and diction.
Also available in *Eighteenth-Century English Eng-
lish Literature: Modern Essays in Criticism.* Ed.
James L. Clifford. New York: Oxford University
Press, 1959, pp. 130-143.

C45 ---. *A Preface to Eighteenth-Century Poetry.* Oxford: Clarendon Press, 1948, pp. 94-95.
Trivia, Pulteney epistle and *Rural Sports* excel
in description, sophisticated, artificial style and burlesque which balances vulgarity and artificiality.

C46 Thackeray, William M. *The English Humorists of the Eighteenth Century.* London: Smith, Elder and Co., 1853. pp. 160-218.

   (Fourth Lecture: Prior, Gay and Pope) Gentleness and playfulness characterizes Gay, as extensive use of Spence's *Anecdotes*, letters and poems show. Gay superior to Philips as a humorist.

C47 Tovey, Duncan C. "John Gay." *Reviews and Essays in English Literature.* 1897; rpt. Port Washington, New York: Kennikat, 1970, pp. 115-137.

   Indulgent review: *Beggar's Opera* coarse compared to Gilbert's works; *Fables* inferior to LaFontaine's and greatest talent is for trivial and detailed. Gay's works who "early symptom of a desire" for little more ease in verse. *Trivia* reveals his true talent.

C48 Underhill, John. "Introductory Memoir." *Poems of John Gay.* London: Routledge, 1893. I, xi-lxix.

   Biographical review with background of publication and performance of works and critical reputation. Lack of independence characterizes Gay when viewed by friends. *Fables* determines his position as a poet.

C49 Warton, Joseph. *An Essay on the Writings and Genius of Pope.* London: Printed for J. Dodsley, 1782, 4th ed. II, 251-254.

   Study of sweetness and simplicity in Gay's works, which lack elevation and spirit. *Fables* inferior to LaFontaine's and *Beggar's Opera* too highly praised for moral effects by Pope and Swift; it will probably only harden pickpockets, strumpets and highwaymen and fostered the monstrous comic opera. Queensberrys suffocated Gay.

C50 Wright, G. W. "Nicholas Rowe." *Notes and Queries,* 21 January 1939, pp. 51-52.

   Censors' removal of Rowe and Gay memorials from Poet's Corner to storage for uninterrupted view of wall paintings in Westminster Abbey.

Rural Sports

D1 Aden, John M. "The 1720 Version of *Rural Sports* and the Georgic Tradition." *Modern Language Quarterly*, 20 (1959), 228-232.
Changes in 1720 version render poem a truer generic piece than 1713 version because structure and subtitle more aligned with Virglian model.

D2 Arthos, John. *The Language of Natural Description in Eighteenth-Century Poetry*. Ann Arbor: The University of Michigan Press, 1949, pp. 136, 231, 260, 300, 329, 372, 386.
Study of diction using quotes from *Rural Sports*.

D3 Chalker, John. "John Gay: 'Rural Sports' and 'Trivia.'" *The English Georgic: A Study in the Development of a Form*. Baltimore: Johns Hopkins Press, 1969, pp. 141-179.
Study of *Rural Sports* as poem of retirement to country, with analysis of Virgilian debts and Gay's distinctive touches of eighteenth-century meditation, Miltonic echoes, poetic diction plus poem's relationship to seventeenth-century fishing manuals, classical and post-classical materials, comic dimension created by epic vocabulary, syntax, Miltonic references, use of fishes to point a moral.

D4 Culbertson, Owen. "Introduction." *"Rural Sports," together with "The Birth of the Squire" and "The hound and the huntsman."* New York: William Rudge, 1930, pp. xi-xxvix.

Study of differences between 1713 and 1720 editions, echoes of *Rural Sports* in Somerville's *The Chace, A Journey to Exeter* and brief career review.

D5 Donovan, Mortimer. "Early Reference to the Dry Fly." *Notes and Queries*, 10 June 1950, p. 247.
In Canto I, Gay's fisherman may be using dry fly; thus, theory that Thomas Barker's *Art of Angling* (1651) contains first ref. to dry fly may be erroneous since the fly in that work seems to be in the water.

D6 Durling, Dwight. *Georgic Tradition in English Poetry*. Port Washington, New York: Kennikat, 1935, pp. 37-39.
Georgic "naturalized" by Dennys, Philips, Tickell and Gay. *Rural Sports* is an offshoot of the georgic and blends three types of field sports.

D7 Røstvig, Maren-Sofie. *The Happy Man, Studies in the Metamorphoses of a Classical Ideal*. Oslo: Oslo University Press, 1954. II, 228-230. Oslo Studies in English, No.7.
Rural Sports combines halieutic, cynegetic and ixeutic traditional with description of seasons and echoes of Horace's second epode, Virgil's first eclogue. "Contemplation on Night" and introductory poem to *Fables* are "physico-theological" and in keeping with *beatus ille* tradition.

The Shepherd's Week

E1 Battestin, Martin. "Menalcas' Song: The Meaning of Art and Artifice in Gay's Poetry." *Journal of English and Germanic Philology,* 65 (October 1966), 662-679.

> Excellent study of how Gay uses pastoral to show Nature must be made to imitate art, to recover ideal lost in actuality but attainable through art. Stylistic devices establish values and control, as comparison to Swift's "City Shower" poem indicates. References are made to *Rural Sports.*

E2 Bond, Richmond P. *English Burlesque Poetry.* Cambridge: Harvard University Press, 1932, pp. 110-115.

> Superficial plot review which grants independent success of rustic pictures and sees *Shepherd's Week* supporting Pope because it burlesques sterile eclogue form: Gay balances burlesque and charm of country portraits.

E3 Burd, Henry A. "The Golden Age Idea in Eighteenth-Century Poetry." *Sewanee Review,* 23 (1915), 172-185.

> "Proeme" is an attempt to "discredit" Pope's view of pastoral as image of Golden Age; this "iconoclasm" is also present in Prologue to *Dione.*

E4 Burgess, C. F. "Scriblerian Influence in 'The Shepherd's Week.'" *Notes and Queries,* 1963, p. 318.

> Appended pseudo-index of alphabetical catalogue of "Names, Plants" and other materials in *Shepherd's Week* burlesques scholarly pedantry in Scriblerus Club tradition.

E5 Congleton, J. E. *Theories of Pastoral Poetry in England, 1684-1798*. Gainesville: University of Florida Press, 1952. See chapters 3 and 4.
> Good review of whole pastoral controversy: Chapter 3 a thorough consideration of Rapin and Fontenelle, Chapter 4 of Neoclassical development and Chapter 5 of Rationalism. Gay burlesques rationalists, though Purney viewed him as serious. Congleton surveys several opinions regarding Gay's purpose in pastorals.

E6 Ellis, William, Jr. "Thomas D'Urfey, the Pope-Philips Quarrel, and *The Shepherd's Week*." *Publications of the Modern Language Association*, 74 (1959), 203-212.
> Careful review of D'Urfey's reputation as rustic songwriter. Gay imitates elements of D'Urfey's songs to mock school of pastoral realism.

E7 Goldsmith, Oliver. *The Beauties of English Poesy*. London: Printed for William Griffin, 1767, p. 133.
> *Shepherd's Week* Gay's "principal performance" because it reflects "true spirit of pastoral poetry" resembling Theocritus more than any other English pastoralist.

E8 Heuston, Edward F. "Gay's Bowzybeus and Thomas D'Urfey." *Scriblerian*, 1 (Autumn 1968), 30-31.
> Bowzybeus' behavior in "Saturday" satirizes "singing and tippling" of D'Urfey.

E9 Jones, Richard F. "Eclogue Types in English Poetry of the Eighteenth Century." *Journal of English and Germanic Philology*, 24 (1925), 33-60.
> Definition and study of eclogue genre with review of classical, French and Renaissance eclogues and Gay's role in Pope-Philips controversy.

E10 Kerlin, Robert Thomas. *Theocritus in English Literature*. Lynchburg, Virginia: J. P. Bell, 1910, pp. 50-59.
> *Shepherd's Week* initially intended as burlesque but sense of reality and feeling toward nature produces pastorals superior to Pope or Philips.

> *Shepherd's Week, Dione, Araminta* and *Acis and Galatea* also contain borrowings from Theocritus.

E11 Kitchin, George. *A Survey of Burlesque and Parody in English.* London: Oliver and Boyd, 1931, pp. 106-108, 118.
> *Shepherd's Week* inspired by Pope and in turn inspired Southey to do *English Eclogues.* Gay had "parasitical talent" which led to parody. Kitchin also discusses *Journey to Exeter* and *Epistle to Mr. Pope.*

E12 Mantz, Harold Elmer. "Non-Dramatic Pastoral in Europe in the Eighteenth Century." *Publications of the Modern Language Association,* n.s. 24 (Sept. 1916), 421-447.
> Pope instigated Gay to write *Shepherd's Week* to ridicule Philips; Gay one of first moderns in pastoral because he made country folk alive even though he did it in caricature.

E13 Moore, John Robert. "Gay's Burlesque of Sir Richard Blackmore's Poetry." *Journal of English and Germanic Philology,* 50 (1951), 83-89.
> Gay burlesques Blackmore's song of Mopas and *Creation* in "Saturday."

E14 Nitchie, Elizabeth. *Vergil and the English Poets.* New York: Columbia University Press, 1919, pp. 173, 174n, 177, 179.
> Scattered references: *Shepherd's Week* probably instigated by Pope, yet may satirize Virgil since burlesque is closer to Latin form than many serious imitations. Nitchie has references to *Trivia* and *Fan* also.

E15 Trowbridge, Hoyt. "Pope, Gay and *The Shepherd's Week.*" *Modern Language Quarterly,* 5 (March 1944), 79-88.
> Best appreciation of Gay's role in pastoral controversy with six categories of Philips-directed parody.

Trivia

F1   Bogorad, Samuel N. "Milton's 'Paradise Lost' and Gay's 'Trivia': A Borrowing." *Notes and Queries*, 4 March 1950, pp. 98-99.

      Description of fire (III, 382-386) verbally parallel to Milton's description of Satan when Ithuriel and Zephon discover him in garden (*P.L.*, iv, 814-819).

F2   Burgess, C. F. "The Ambivalent Point of View in John Gay's *Trivia*." *Cithara*, 4 (1964), 53-65.

      Persona's satiric and sympathetic responses create ambivalence which is both burlesque and accurate guide to London.

F3   Chalker, John. "John Gay: 'Rural Sports' and 'Trivia.'" *The English Georgic: A Study in the Development of a Form*. Baltimore: Johns Hopkins Press, 1969, pp. 141-179.

      Trivia can be compared to Juvenal's Third Satire: Juvenal's indignation replaced by Gay's enjoyment and skill. Experience is fused with "day-to-day activities," so that not mock epic but didactic and descriptive prevails with comic echoes of *Georgics*.

F4   Durling, Dwight. *Georgic Tradition in English Poetry*. Port Washington, New York: Kennikat, 1935, pp. 35-39.

      Trivia is a broad parody of georgic themes in a modern British frame.

F5　Ellis, Stewart Marsh. "John Gay and London." *Mainly Victorian.* London: Hutchinson, pp. 287-291.
　　　(Reprinted in collection of essays; originally in *Fortnightly Review* of April 1923) *Trivia* depicts Hogarthian orientation to London.

F6　Goad, Caroline. "John Gay." *Horace in the English Literature of the Eighteenth Century.* New Haven: Yale University Press, 1918; rpt. New York: Haskell House, 1967, pp. 116-127.
　　　Catalogues major borrowings from Horace.

F7　Kernan, Alvin B. "The Magnifying Tendency: Gay's *Trivia; or The Art of Walking the Streets of London.*" *The Plot of Satire.* New Haven: Yale University Press, 1965, pp. 36-50.
　　　Stylistic inflation and amplification satirize dullness of walker: Gay also uses epic devices applied to unsuitable subjects, sentimentality and maxims. Overall, irony is mild and Horatian. Kernan admits to treating walker more seriously than Gay.

F8　Lilly, Marie Loretto. *The Georgic, A Contribution to the Study of the Vergilian Type of Didactic Poetry.* Baltimore: Johns Hopkins Press, 1919, pp. 43, 49, 124-127. Hesperia-Supplement Series: Studies in English Philology, No. 6.
　　　Trivia a georgic burlesque; *Receipt for Stewing Veal* prosaic, a non-Vergilian bit of rhyme with advice. *Rural Sports* a "mediocre" cynegetica which doesn't have earlier works on chase in mind.

F9　Mustard, W. P. "Virgil's Georgics and the British Poets." *American Journal of Philology,* 29 (1908), 1-32.
　　　Superceded by other discussions. *Trivia* is a "cheap" imitation of Swift's "City Shower" poem.

F10　Probyn, Clive T. "Swift's Borrowing from Gay." *Notes and Queries,* May 1969, p. 184.
　　　Cloacina's giving of birth to shoe boy (II, 140-142) like Swift's scene of shoe-boy in *On Poetry: A Rapsody* (1733), 11. 33, 35-36.

F11- Sherbo, Arthur. "Virgil, Dryden, Gay and Matters Trivial."
       Publications of the Modern Language Association, 85
       (October 1970), 1063-1070.
           Distinguishes Gay from walker and demonstrates
           that Spacks' too-serious interpretation ignores Gay's
           dependence on Dryden's translation of Virgil. Gay's
           blend of elements from many sources results in suc-
           cessful mock flavor.

F12 "*Trivia* and *Polly* by John Gay." *Times Literary Supplement*,
       27 July 1922, p. 489.
           Hammersmith revival prompts republishing of *Trivia*
           quarto with Hogarth prints and without "silly"
           Cloacina tale omitted from first edition.

Fables

* G1 *Brice's Weekly Journal,* 12 April 1728.
  Contains essay on Fable 18.

G2 Bryce, John C. " 'Addition' to Gay's Fables." *Times Literary Supplement,* 4 July 1935, p. 432.
  Issues inquiry about copy of pamphlet titled "A Tale being an Addition to Mr. Gay's *Fables*" and quotes from Ramsay's *Life of Cyrus* (Dublin, 1728.)

G3 Dobson, Austin. "Gay's Fables." *Modern English Essays.* London: J. M. Dent and Sons; New York: E. P. Dutton, 1922. II, 32-49.
  Reviews life, with emphasis on political interests and relationship with Queensberrys; very brief consideration of *Fables,* which despite faults are full of good sense, wisdom and observation.

G4 Graham, Edwin. "John Gay's Second Series, the *Craftsman* in Fables." *Papers on Language and Literature,* 5 (Winter 1969), 17-25.
  Second series of *Fables,* like *Beggar's Opera* and *Polly,* are opposition satire aimed at Walpole; in them Gay uses standard allusions to corruption which were used by Tory press.

* G5 Murakami, Shiko. "On John Gay's *Fables.*" *Studies in English Literature by the English Lit. Society of Japan,* 19 (1939), 494-503.

* G6   Plessow, Max. *Geschichte der fabehtichtung in English bis zu John Gay.* Berlin: Mayert Müller, 1906.
Study of *Fables* (In German).

G7   Wells, Henry W. "The Seven Against London, A Study in the Satirical Tradition of Augustan Poetry." *Sewanee Review,* 47 (October-December 1939), 514-523.
Study in verse format: Augustan satire, includes *Fables.*

Other Poetical Works

H1 Aitken, George A. "Gay's Chair," *The Academy*, 18 May
    1895, pp. 426-427.
        Alterations in "The Maid's Petition" copy available
        in manuscript; also, mention of prefix to "Licentia
        Poetica discuss'd."

H2 ---. "Pamphlets by John Gay." *The Athenaeum*, 7 September
    1889, pp. 321-322.
        Examines pieces Gay published under pseud. Sir
        James Barker: "God's Revenge Against Punning"
        (1716), "An Admonition . . . to Mr. Trapp" (1717) and
        a pamphlet to Steele (1718).

H3 Ault, Norman. "Mr. Pope's 'Poetical soop': evidence of
    authorship.'" *Times Literary Supplement*, 3 June 1944,
    p. 276.
        Pope's poem on stewed veal his own but probably
        handwirtten by Gay due to Pope's injured hand;
        perhaps Swift misread the ms. and assumed Gay the
        author.

H4 Ball, F. Elrington. "Gay's Works." *Notes and Queries*,
    3 March 1923, p. 174.
        Notes: (1) regards Gay's authorship of "Newgate's
        Garland." (2) gives location of Molly Mog and note
        on "Sweet William's Farewell."

H5 ---. *Swift's Verse, An Essay*. London: John Murray, 1929.
    See index for many references in passing.

(p. 209) Swift's "peculiar turn of thought" quite visible in "Molly Mog."

(p. 190) "Blueskin's Ballad" under title "Newgate's Garland" with variations has been attributed to Gay but probably is Swift's.

(p. 199) Quidnunckis poem attributed to Gay but belongs to Swift.

* H6   Baller, Joseph. *Gay's Chair; Poems Never Before Printed*, 1819.
> Previously unprinted poem edition includes introductory memoir.

H7   Barnett, George L. "Gay, Swift, and 'Tristram Shandy.'" *Notes and Queries*, 4 December 1943, pp. 346-347.
> Pope-Gay poem "Receipt for Stewing Veal" appears in first part of Sterne's novel.

H8   Beattie, Lester M. "The Authorship of The Quidnunckis." *Modern Philology*, 30 (February 1933), 317-320.
> 1724 poem addressed to Quidnuncs often attributed to Pope, Gay or Arbuthnot but belongs to Arbuthnot because it resembles his "characteristic sentiment" and "economical prose style."

* H9   Brie, Frederick. *English Rokoko-Epik (1710-1730)*. Munich: Hueber, 1927.
> Discusses *Fan* and other minor pieces.

H10   Burgess, C. F. "Gay's 'Twas When the Seas Were Roaring'" and Chaucer's 'Franklin's Tale': A Borrowing." *Notes and Queries*, December 1962, pp. 454-455.
> Ribaldry of Gay's *Wife of Bath* meant to capture earthiness of Chaucer; fourth stanza of Gay's ballad parallels Dorigen's soliloquy in "Franklin's Tale."

H11   ---. "Mr. Gay, Amanuensis." *Notes and Queries*, August 1964, p. 293.
> Confirms Pope's authorship of "Veal" recipe by examining letter (September 1726) to Edward Harley.

H12 Butt, John. "A Prose Fragment Wrongly Attributed to Gay and Pope." *Notes and Queries*, January 1955, pp. 23-25.

> Fragment relating a dream was inspired by allegorical vision in *Spectator* No. 159. A letter from Gay to Fortescue and validity of Fortescue's handwriting confirm Gay's authorship in 1713.

H13 Dearing, Vinton A. "John Gay: Two Corrections." *Scriblerian*, 1 (Spring 1969), 32.

> Gay's letter to Addison (December 1713) is actually to Addison's stepson, based on evidence of subscription to 1720 poetry collection. The date of journey in "A Journey to Exeter" is July 1716 because Septennial Act and rebuilding of Burglinton's houses occurred in 1716.

H14 Edwards, Ralph. "Gay's Chair: A Possible Link with the 'Beggar's Opera.'" *Country Life*, 3 April 1926, pp. 508-509.

> Mostly fascinated with chair as a piece of furniture; includes history, description, a few lines of poetry found in chair and completely unfounded speculation that some of *Beggar's Opera* may have been written in chair.

H15 Forsgren, Adina. "Gay Among the Defenders of the Faith." *Studia Neophilologica*, 38 (1966), 301-313.

> Informed background study in which "Contemplation on Night" and "Thought on Eternity" found to support orthodox religion with his emphasis on "low" kinds.

H16 ---. "Lofty Genii and Low Ghosts. Vision Poems and John Gay's 'True Story of an Apparition.'" *Studia Neophilologica*, 40 (1968), 197-215.

> Extensive background study finds Gay's poem a Scriblerian answer to "high-flown Whig visions with guardian angels."

H17 ---. "Some Complimentary Epistles by John Gay." *Studia*

Neophilologica, 36 (1964), 82-100.
Gay's epistles generally homelier and more realistic
than their Horatian models. "Epistle to a Lady"
features "low" eulogy of the common-place, like
epistle on George I's accession to throne. In epistles,
Gay varies modes of imitation to create "modern
psychological" rather than neo-classical method.

H18 Havens, Raymond D. *The Influence of Milton on English
Poetry.* New York: Russell and Russell, 1961, pp. 15,
107, 623-633.
Labels *Wine* as humorous imitation of *Paradise Lost;*
corrects error that *Verses under the Picture of Blackmore* was written by Swift and lists *Rural Sports* as
rhymed technical treatise of Milton.

H19 Kroeber, Karl. *Romantic Narrative Art.* Madison: University
of Wisconsin Press, 1960, pp. 21-24.
Gay reduces narrative to single scene with rhyme
and craftsmanship and thus transforms ballad art
into "polished, stingingly ironic verse."

H20 Lucas, Edward V. "Maids of the Inn." *Pleasure Trove.*
New York: Lippincott, 1935, pp. 165-174.
Considers Swift and Pope's assistance in "Molly
Mog" and later Molly-maid poems.

H21 M., M. "Molly Mog." *Notes and Queries,* 30 July 1859, pp.
84-85.
Rose Inn, where Molly Mog written, now mercer's
shop. Marry Mogg of Oakingham is probably the
Molly of the song and Edward Stand the swain.

H22 McLeod, A. L. "Notes on John Gay." *Notes and Queries,*
20 January 1951, pp. 32-34.
Several notes: (1) Letter in *Gentleman's Magazine*
(1738) under pseud. Pamphilus is by Dr. Johnson.
(2) Hint by Swift of *Beggar's Opera* in letter (30
August 1716) to Pope predates suggestion recorded
in Spence's *Anecdotes.* (3) Gay, not Pope, author of
famous letter on death of two lovers by lightening.

(4) Character names in *Distress'd Wife* resemble Congreve's dramatic technique; perhaps Congreve assisted because first three acts superior to second two.

H23 ---. "Pope and Gay: Two Overlooked Manuscripts." *Notes and Queries*, August 1953, pp. 334-337.
> Study of Fortescue letter and prose composition on a dream, Gay's letter to Fortescue and a sample from *Fan*.

H24 Mayhew, George P. "A Draft of Ten Lines from Swift's Poem to John Gay." *John Rylands Library Bulletin*, 37 (September 1954), 257-262.
> Discussion of prosody of different versions of 1731 poem to Gay in supposed capacity of treasurer to Duke of Queensberry; later developed into attack on Walpole.

H25 Montetiore, Arthur. " 'Coridon's Song,' and Other Verse from Various Sources." *The Athenaeum*, 1 December 1894, p. 752.
> Corrects error that village in "Journey to Exeter" is Morecombe-Lake; really Charmouth according to topographical details and tradition of lobster-catching.

H26 Osborn, James M. " 'That on Whiston,' by John Gay." *Publications of Bibliographical Society of America*, 56 (1962), 73-78.
> Spence anecdote in which Pope credits Gay with authorship of "Ode for Musick" (1727) probably refers to "A True and Faithful Narrative" (1729 or 1730), a satire on Whiston.

H27 Potter, Alfred C. "Gay's Works." *Notes and Queries*, 7 April 1923, 273.
> Notes on "Newfate's Garland," "M. Mogg," and "Sweet William's Farewell."

H28 Rawson, C. J. "Parnell on Whiston." *The Papers of the Bibliographical Society of America*, 57 (First Quarter, 1963), 91-92.

Reference in letter (23 December 1714) from Richard Cox to Edward Southwell calls Parnell author of "Ode for Musick" which Osborn suggested Gay did not author.

H29 ---. "A Phrase of John Gay in Swift's *Modest Defence of the Lady's Dressing-Room?*"

Swift possibly saw Gay's letter to Parnell (March 1716) because phrase "voids out worms of monstrous size" in poem echoes letter.

H30 Robinson, Disney. "Fly Leaves, No. 32." *Gentleman's Magazine*, 96a (September 1826), 230-231.

Isaac Reed marked three poems as forgeries in 1723 edition printed for John Bell.

H31 Rosenberg, Albert. "The Date of John Gay's 'An Epistle to Burlington.'" *Philological Quarterly*, 30 (January 1951), 94-96.

Advertisement in *Daily Courant* (18 February 1717) gives proof of proper date. Pope's letter to Jervas mentioned Gay's attack on Blackmore for Swift. Sherburn credits Gay with anonymous *Verses on England's Arch-Poet*, though the dating is unsure.

H32 Teske, Charles B. "Gay's 'Twas when the Seas were Roaring' and the Rise of Pathetic Balladry." *Anglia*, 83 (1965), 411-425.

Study of ballad's parody of conventional pastoral and broadside elements, rejecting both too-serious and too-mocking interpretations; also includes a comparison of Gay's ballad to Rowe's "Colin's Complaint" and Prior's "The Despairing Shepherd."

H33 Thomas, W. Moy. "Alpieu: Lady Mary Wortley Montagu's 'Town Eclogues.'" *Notes and Queries*, 28 June 1890, p. 515.

Pope told Spence "Lydia" ("The Toilette") is almost wholly Gay's, with five or six new lines by Montagu, though some thought Pope himself the author.

H34 Williams, Harold. "The Canon of Swift." *Review of English Studies*, 3 (April 1927) , 212-213.
> Supports Ball's contention that Swift wrote Quidnuncki's poem.

H35 ---. "To a Lady on Her Passion for Old China." *Review of English Studies*, 7 (January 1931), 79-80.
> Advertisements in *Daily Courant* (12 May 1725) and *Daily Post* (13 May) plus publication in 1767 edition of *Poems on Several Occasions* confirm Faber's dating of poem.

H36 Williams, Iolo A. "John Gay: An Overlooked Poem." *London Mercury*, 7 (April 1923), 636-637.
> Corrects Melville's note that Gay wrote nothing between 1708 and 1711: in 1709 his preface to William Coward's *Licentia Poetica Discuss'd* appeared.

H37 Winton, Calhoun. "John Gay and a Devon Jug." *Winterthur Portfolio*, 2 (1965), 62-64.
> North Devon jug with date 1698 bears verse inscription which may be work of thirteen-year-old Gay; spirit of lines appears in later ballad and *Shepherd's Week* and interest in decorative arts demonstrated in "To a Lady on her Passion for Old China."

H38 Yeowell, J. "Molly Mog." *Notes and Queries*, 27 August 1859, pp. 172-175.
> Concerns attempts to determine authorship of M. M.; among them Swift's 1729 statement that Gay was author. Yeowell also includes obituary note on M. M.'s father.

The Beggar's Opera

I1 Agate, James. "A View of *The Beggar's Opera.*" *Alarums and Excursions*. London: Grant Richards, 1922, pp. 139-152.

>Review of Hazlitt's criticism that Americans can't understand *Beggar's Opera* and how Gay glossed over Polly's "wantonness." Agate also includes comparison to Fielding's rogues and superficial review of acting in Hammersmith revival.

* I2 Andrews, Hilda J. "John Gay and English Ballad Opera." *Music Teacher* (October 1927), 620-621.

I3 Angelo, Henry. *The Reminiscences of Henry Angelo*. London: Kegan, Paul, Trubner and Co., 1830. I, 25-26.

>Credits satire against court for play's success, though Pope's more spirited wit "charged" much of the opera. Pope altered last two lines of Peachum's first song and lines in Macheath's sons, "Since laws were made for every degree."

I4 Baker, David. *Biographica Dramatica; or, a companion to the Playhouse*. London: Printed for Longman and Others, 1782. I, 184-187.

>Biographical review with interest in court attempts, low-life intentions and ridicule of Italian drama. V. II contains alphabetical list of plays, dates and brief comment on importance of each.

* I5   Banerjie, Santi Ranjan. *"The Beggar's Opera* and the Comic
        Tradition." *Bulletin of the Department of English (Cal-
        cutta University)*, 4 (1968-1969), 51-54.

  I6   Baring, Maurice. "The Beggar's Opera." *The New States-
        man*, 12 June 1920, pp. 279-280.
            Includes Pope's statements on opening night and
            Dr. Johnson's on novelty. English music provides
            vitality and Baring hopes for revival of Hammersmith
            production.

  I7   Berger, A. V. *"The Beggar's Opera*, the burlesque, and
        Italian Opera." *Music and Letters*, 17 (April 1936),
        93-105.
            Reviews criticisms of satire and burlesque, in tradi-
            tion of *Rehearsal* with borrowed arias and folk
            melodies as Gay's particular contribution.

  I8   Blom, Eric. *Music in England.* New York: Penguin Books,
        1942, pp. 107, 124-130, 135, plus references in
        passing.
            Beggar's Opera harmed Italian opera, but *Polly*
            "feebler." Ramsay's 1725 *Gentle Shepherd* unlike
            1729 ballad-operatized version. Blom also mentions
            Acis and Galatea.

  I9   Boswell, James. *Boswell's Life of Johnson, Together with
        Boswell's Journal of a Tour to the Hebrides and Johnson's
        Diary of a Journey into North Wales.* Ed. George Birbeck
        Hill; revised by L. F. Powell, Oxford: Clarendon Press,
        1934. Volumes II, III, IV, V.
            II, 367-379: *Beggar's Opera* never made rogue of
            anyone yet made character of rogue familiar and
            "in some degree pleasing." It is such a "labe-
            factation" of all principles to be injurious to
            morality, yet Johnson would be sorry to see it
            suppressed. He also comments on Quin's reluc-
            tance to play Macheath and Queensberry's attitude.
            II, 442 (20 March 1776): The robber who reasons as
            the gang in *Beggar's Opera* is still object of indig-
            nation.

> III, 198 (23 September 1777): Airs in *Beggar's Opera* never fail to recommend Gay.
>
> III, 321 (23 April 1778): Burke thinks play has no merit; Johnson thought its novelty alone might carry it.
>
> V, 289 (5 October 1773): Johnson comments on line "As men should serve a cucumber."

* I10 *Bristol News*, 11 May 1728.

I11 Brockway, Wallace and Herbert Weinstock. "Handel." *Opera; A History of Its Creation and Performance: 1660-1941.* New York: Simon and Schuster, 1941, pp. 41-42.
>
> *Beggar's Opera* caused audiences to desert regular opera. Pepusch's sole original contribution was overture, despite claims he adapted many songs.

I12 Bronson, Bertrand. *"The Beggar's Opera." Studies in the Comic.* Berkeley: University of California Publications in English, 8, 2 (1941), 197-231.
>
> Examines probable parodies of Handel's works and concludes that satire not viscious but merely pokes fun at Italian conventions. Lyrics feature ironic and witty matchings of words and tunes; characters themselves possess qualities which extend satiric message that all are alike.
>
> > Also available in *Facets of the Enlightenment, Studies in English Literature and Its Contents.* Berkeley: University of California, 1968, pp. 60-90. Also available in *Studies in the Literature of the Augustan Age.* Ed. Richard C. Boys. Ann Arbor: George Wahr, 1952.

I13 Brydges, E. T. *"The Beggar's Opera." Notes and Queries,* 29 June 1895, pp. 501-502.
>
> Concerns Chancery suit involving *Beggar's Opera* copyright; also mentions suits on other works.

* I14 Burgess, C. F. "The Genesis of *The Beggar's Opera.*" *Cithara,* 2 (1962), 6-12.

I15 ---. "Political Satire: John Gay's *The Beggar's Opera.*"
  Midwest Quarterly, 6 (1965), 265-276.
> Outline of political satire, particularly Macheath
> and Peachum functions. The beggar-statesman unity
> was formed early in Gay's *What d'ye Call It* (1715),
> a 1723 letter to Mrs. Howard, the Old Bailey Trial
> (1727), and Gay's own political disappointment (1727).

I16 Burney, Charles. *A General History of Music From the Ear-
  liest Years to the Present (1789).* New York: Dover, 1957.
> (First printed in 1782) Pepusch credited for writing
> overture and "wild, rude, and often vulgar melodies"
> with excellent bases. 1727 burlesque, *Dragon of
> Wantley*, by Carey is a more successful ridicule of
> Italian opera than *Beggar's Opera.* Burney reprints
> Arbuthnot's letter which hails play as "touch-stone
> to try British taste on," at last uncovering true Brit-
> ish inclinations.

I17 Bushnell, Margaret. "Gay's Satirical Method." *Asides* (1942),
  22-24.
> Study of Peachum's attitudes toward marriage, custom
> and fashion, Macheath's attitudes, and Polly's role
> as straight character in play burlesque world.

* I18 Calmus, J. "Die Beggar's Opera von Gay und Pepusch."
  Sammelbände der Internationalen Musikgesellschaft,
  8 (1906).

I19 Carr, Comyns. " 'The Beggar's Opera' in the Eighteenth
  Century." *Blackwood's Magazine*, 211 (June 1922),
  790-797.
> Review of events prior to production and play's
> relationship to Italian opera. Carr pictures opening
> night, with Queensberrys, Walpole and Polly being
> emphasized.

I20 Cibber, Colley. *An Apology for the Life of Mr. Colley Cibber.*
  London: Printed for John Watts, 1753, p. 141.
> Confesses Gay successful because he gratified
> public taste and concentrates on problems of *Polly.*

I21 Coeuroy, André. *"Le Beggar's Opera* à Paris." *Revue Anglo-Américaine*, 1 (October 1923), 62-65.
 Review of satire with focus on music. (In French)

I22 Coke, Lady Mary. *The Letters and Journals of Lady Mary Coke*. Bath: Kingsmead Reprints, IV (1772-1774), 136-137.
 Brief account of Sir John Fielding's attempt to keep *Beggar's Opera* off stage; if acted, Fielding wanted Macheath executed.

I23 Colles, Henry C. "That Pick-Pocket Opera." *Essays and Lectures*. London: Oxford University Press, 1945, pp. 52-54.
 Imagines meeting when evil of *Beggar's Opera* discussed by Fielding, Handel and others.

I24 Cooke, William. *Memoirs of Charles Macklin*. London: Printed for James Asperne, 1806, 2nd ed., pp. 27-67.
 Background of actors, including first cast; also includes notes on satire, writers of songs and moral problem.

I25 Courthorpe. *A History of English Poetry*. London: Macmillan, 1911. V, 440.
 Beggar's Opera a combination of comedy and opera and its success due to Gay's awareness of public taste.

* I26 Craig, Edward G. *"The Beggar's Opera."* *Mask*, 12 (January 1926), opposite page 1.

* I27 *Daily Courant*, 1 February 1728.

* I28 *Daily Gazeteer*, 7 May 1737 (open letter).

* I29 *Daily Journal*, 1 February 1728.

* I30 *Daily Post*, 22 May 1728.

I31 Dent, Edward J. *Foundations of English Opera, A Study of Musical Drama in England During the Seventeenth Century.* New York: DaCapo, 1965, p. 146n.

> Gay possibly influenced by Duffett's prison parodies when he wrote his opera, though it is not necessarily a direct source.

I32 Donaldson, Ian. "'A Double Capacity': *The Beggar's Opera.*" *The World Upside Down, Comedy from Johnson to Fielding.* Oxford: Clarendon Press, 1970, pp. 159-182.

> Gay invites us to see both callous and "soft-hearted" in Macheath, plus the whole gang: this combination allows us to see Hobbesian scepticism and Shaftesburian optimism.

I33 Dodds, M. H. "*The Beggar's Opera* in Dickens." *Notes and Queries,* 7 January 1922, p. 14.

> *Beggar's Opera* incorporates two quotes from *Old Curiosity Shop* and *Our Mutual Friend.* C. W. B. replies (28 January 1922 *Notes and Queries*) that references are dramatic and popular, not literary; he also adds one reference in *David Copperfield* For the remainder of 1922, *Notes and Queries* contains correspondence on literary uses of Dickens by other authors.

* I34 Drâghici, Simona. "'The Beggar's Opera' de John Gay si lumea parddoxului. Studii despre teztrul univèrsal. *Studii de literatură universală,* 10, 27-34.

> Study of paradox.

I35 Dramaticus. "Receipts to the Beggar's Opera on its Production." *Notes and Queries,* 19 January 1950, pp. 178-179.

> Examines receipts at Lincoln's Inn Fields, including Gay's share.

I36 Duff, E. G. "Art and Crime." *The London Mercury,* 5 (February 1922), 413-414.

> Correspondence reveals Walpole's letter (4 November 1773) to Horace Mann which relates Justice Fielding's

revival of theory that play responsible for roguery.

137 Empson, William. "The Beggar's Opera, Mock-Pastoral
as the Cult of Independence." *Some Versions of Pastoral.* New York: New Directions, 1960.
In lengthy discussion of double plots, Empson
examines how mixture of heroic and pastoral conven-
tions and delicate uses of diction create satire.
Thieves and whores parody aristocratic ideal, while
Locket and thief-catcher parody bourgeois ideal.

* 138 *Evening Post,* 1 February 1728.

139 Firkins, Oliver W. " 'The Beggar's Opera' and Its Progenry."
Weekly Review, 16 February 1921, pp. 161-163.
Compares Gay to Gilbert and considers typical of-
fenses of musical comedy (includes notes on Green-
which Village revival).

140 Flood, W. H. Grattan. "First Ballad Opera: Ramsay's 'Gentle
Shepherd' or the 'Beggar's Opera.' " *Musical Times,* 1024
(June 1928), 554-555.
Corrects Kidson's claim that Ramsay never saw Gay's
opera performed; he did on 22 January 1729. Gay probably influenced by 1726 visit to Ramsay and in 1727
based *Beggar's Opera* on Ramsay's libretto scheme.

141 Gagey, Edmond McAdoo. *"The Beggar's Opera and Polly."*
Ballad Opera. New York: Benjamin Blom, 1937, pp.
35-52.
Thorough study of ballad opera as dramatic genre
and comprehensive bibliography of ballad operas.
Elizabethan jig and French *comedie en vaudeville*
are probable sources, plus early low-life plays,
serious and comic opera. Gagey defers to Schultz
and Pearce for specific discussions of *Beggar's
Opera,* but does review facts of production and
acting history, plus satires on political figures,
Italian opera, stock romance and play's influence
on genre of ballad opera.

142 Genest, John. *Some Account of the English Stage From the Restoration in 1660 to 1830.* Bath: Printed for M. E. Carrinton, 1932. III.

    Entry for *Beggar's Opera* stresses ridicule of Italian musical drama, retells some of Spence's *Anecdotes* and Swift's commendation of play's morality, Johnson's insistence that play lacks moral purpose, 1772 letter of John Fielding on morality and comments on edition during the playing time through 19 June 1728.

143 Gentleman, Francis. "'The Beggar's Opera': Eighteenth Century." *Specimens of English Dramatic Criticism, XVII-XX Centuries.* London: Oxford University Press, 1945, pp. 69-83.

    (Originally printed in *The Dramatic Censor; or, Critical Companion* [1770].) Review of plot and satire with emphasis on characters and Drury Lane; concludes there is scarcely any moral in *Beggar's Opera*.

* 144 Gibbon. *Old England: or, The Constitutional Journal,* 12 February 1743, p. 9.

    Suggests play brought refinement in thieves' manners.

145 Gilbert, Veddar M. "Unrecorded Comments on John Gay, Henry Travers, and Others." *Notes and Queries,* August 1953, pp. 337-339.

    Insignificant: examines several letters by Thomas Edwards of Terrick to John Clerke; one (21 February 1727) praises burlesque of *Beggar's Opera*.

* 146 *Glouchester Journal,* 16 July 1728.

147 Goberman, Max. "Mr. John Gay's *The Beggar's Opera*." *The Music Review,* 24 (1963), 3-12.

    Commemorative essay which reviews standard background, plot. Songs underscore scenes and sum up emotions, but most limited to charm. Pepusch wrote "rather humdrum figured bases."

148 Goulding, Sybil. "Eighteenth Century French Taste and *The Beggar's Opera*." *Modern Language Review,* 24 (1929), 276-293.

(Quotes in French) Reviews French horror at gross English taste and appearance of English works, including *Beggar's Opera*, on French stage. French translations of Gay's play usually not faithful because of morality problem.

* I49 Granville-Barker, Frank. "John Gay and the Opera." *Halle* (September 1950).

* I50 Harewood, Earl of. *"The Beggar's Opera." Taw and Torridge Festival Programme Book* (1953).

I51 Hawkins, Sir John. *A General History of the Science and Practice of Music.* New York: Dover, 1963. II, 874-877. (Original edition 1853) *Beggar's Opera* motivated more by Gay's political misfortunes than Swift's suggestion. Common speech, ballads and dances disqualify it as an opera. Hawkins concludes violence has been on increase since the play.

I52 ---. "On the Dangerous Tendency of *The Beggar's Opera*." *The Universal Magazine*, 60 (January 1777), 47-48. Political disappointment motivated *Beggar's Opera;* Gay preferred "life of ease and servile dependence on the bounty of his friends, the caprice of the town." The play itself injurious to society and caused violence.

I53 Hazlitt, William. *"The Beggar's Opera:* Nineteenth Century." *Specimens of English Dramatic Criticism, XVII-XX Centuries.* Ed. A. C. Ward. London: Oxford University Press, 1945, pp. 93-95. (Originally in *Morning Chronicle*, 23 October 1813) Reviews particular production of play and discusses its qualities of instruction and delight, though scenes and characters are of the lowest kind; moral purpose gives "force, truth and locality of real feeling to the thoughts and expressions, without being called to the bar of false taste and affected delicacy."

I54 Herbert, A. P. "Preface." *The Beggar's Opera by John Gay,*

John Gay

with an Introduction by A. P. Herbert and Illustrations
by Mariette Lydis. New York: The Heritage Press, 1937,
pp. vii-xviii.
> Social picture of play delights Herbert and reminds
> him of 1732 Proceedings of London Sessions. He
> also includes a sketch by a modern prisoner which
> shares the same theme of thief's honesty.

I55 ---. *Mr. Gay's London.* London: Ernest Benn, 1948.
> Very little about *Beggar's Opera;* primarily extracts
> from 1732-1733 Proceedings at Sessions of the Peace,
> and comments on Newgate life.

I56 ---. "The London of *The Beggar's Opera.*" *Mercury,* 5
(December 1921), 156-171.
> Includes material which appears in his 1948 book.

* I57 Herring, The Rev. Thomas. *Mist's Weekly Journal,* 30 March
1728.
> Denounces *Beggar's Opera* as an immoral work which
> provokes crime.
> See also *Letters from Dr. Herring to William Duncombe.*
>> London, 1777, p. 3, Notes and Appendix.
> Also available in *Seven Sermons on Public Occasions*
>> *by Dr. Herring.* London, 1763, pp. v-xvi.
> See also *London Journal,* 30 March and 20 April 1728.

I58 Hewlett, Maurice Henry. "The Ballad-touch." *Extemporary
Essays.* London: Oxford University Press, 1922, pp.
47-51.
> Little about *Beggar's Opera:* apart from music itself
> songs are worth little. Hewlett reviews songs in
> Shakespeare mostly.

* I59 Heynen, Walter. "The Beggar's Opera." *Masken,* Jahrgang
23 (1929), 21-27.

* I60 Hibbert, H. G. *London Society,* 50 (1886), 16.
> (Article on *Beggar's Opera*) Includes quote from
> *Somerset House Gazette* on conversation between

48

Handel and Pepusch and acting notes (Cited in Irving, *John Gay*, pp. 242-246).

161 Hogarth, George. *Memoirs of the Opera in Italy, France, Germany and England*. London: Richard Bentley, 1851. II, 1-20.

Denies any ridicule of Italian drama and music in *Beggar's Opera*, gives account of Walpole-Townshend quarrel, discusses original actors and reviews moral controversy using opinions by Swift, Sir John Fielding and Dr. Johnson. Polly is only pure character and despite attempts to purify the play, it may die because of its "licentiousness." Hogarth also cites *Polly* and *Acis and Galatea*.

* 162 Höhne, Horst. "John Gay's *Beggar's Opera und Polly*." *Zeitschrift für Anglistik und Amerikanistik*, 13 (1965), 232-260.

(In German) Teil I: Philosophical and aesthetic analysis of *Beggar's Opera* and *Polly*. Teil II [13 (1965), 341-359]: Discussion of irony, wit, satire and humor in *Polly* and *Beggar's Opera*.

* 163 ---. "John Gay's Bühneneverke in Verhältnis *zum* zeitgenössischen Dramenschaffen." *Wissenschaftliche Zeitschrift der Humboldt-Universität zu Berlin*, 11 (1962), 150.

164 Hughes, Charles W. "John Christopher Pepusch." *The Musical Quarterly*, 31 (January 1945), 54-70.

Brief biography and career review of Pepusch. Pope and Swift helped with suggestions; as ballad opera the play is preceded by Ramsay's "Faithful Shepherd." Pepusch is more responsible for work than usually credited.

165 Hunting, Robert S. "How Much is a Cowcumber Worth." *Notes and Queries*, (January 1953), pp. 28-29.

"As Men Should Serve a Cowcumber" (Air vii) not in D'Urfey original; probably a common simile to indicate worthlessness, based on similar uses by

Boswell and *Independent London Journal*. (N.B.: Angus Easson in "Dr. Johnson and the Cucumber: The Question of Value" in *Notes and Queries*, [August 1970], pp. 300-302 responds to Hunting's note by examining Dr. Johnson and others' acquaintance with the term.)

* 166 Hussey, D. "Opera Zebracza J. Gay'a Wczoraj i dzis." *Glos Anglii* (Cracow), 51 (1948), 10.

167 "In Defence." *New Statesman*, 13 May 1922, pp. 146-147.
Responds to Maurice Hewlett's calling the play "decadent."

168 Jaggard, William. "*The Beggar's Opera*." *Notes and Queries*, 2 June 1945, p. 241.
Corrects J. Agate's citation of Pepusch as composer on first edition copy; also reprints part of 1822 Edinburgh critic's statements.

169 "John Gay of 'The Beggar's Opera.'" *The Etude*, 42 (July 1924), 462.
Excerpt from S. Baring Gould's *Devonshire Characters and Strange Events* on opening and financial success.

170 Kern, Jean B. "A Note on *The Beggar's Opera*." *Philological Quarterly*, 18 (1938), 411-413.
Theory that Peachum-Lockit quarrel in II, x parodies Walpole's argument with brother-in-law Lord Townshend is chronologically impossible because the play was written in late 1727, while dispute occurred in 1729.

* 171 "A Key to the Beggar's Opera." *The Craftsman*, 17 February 1728.

172 Kidson, Frank. *The Beggar's Opera: Its Predecessors and Successors*. New York: Macmillan, 1922; rpt. Johnson Rpt. Co., 1969.
Superceded by Schultz's book because it lacks his comprehensive research: reviews opera in England prior to *Beggar's Opera;* calls Ramsay's *Gentle*

Shepherd first ballad opera; reviews Gay's career, plot, characters, and songs. He includes a brief chapter on *Polly;* also history of editions of *Beggar's Opera* with notes on performances and critical reactions.

Rev. in *Contemporary Review,* 122 (September 1921), 402-403.

Rev. in *Notes and Queries,* 26 August 1922, p. 179.

Rev. in *Times Literary Supplement,* 17 August 1922.

173 Knotts, Walter E. "Press Numbers as a Bibliographical Tool, A Study of Gay's *The Beggar's Opera,* 1728." *Harvard Library Bulletin,* 3 (1949), 198-212.

Using first edition of *Beggar's Opera* Knotts concludes small numbers at foot of some pages of eighteenth-century books identify formes of sheet worked off any other press than the one doing bulk of job.

174 Lawrence, W. J. "Early Irish Ballad Opera and Comic Opera." *Musical Quarterly,* 8 (July 1922), 397-412.

Few references to Gay: Bickerstaffe's *Love in a Village* (1762) was first comic opera. After *Beggar's Opera* received lukewarm reception in Dublin, Charles Coffey penned first Irish ballad opera (1729).

175 ---. "Music and Song in the Eighteenth Century Theatre." *The Musical Quarterly,* 2 (January 1916), 67-75.

Though lacks any real discussion of *Beggar's Opera,* a good background work which reviews history of preliminary music and practice of reading words of songs before singing them, using mostly evidence from pre-*Beggar's Opera* works. Eighteenth-century audience surprised at lack of opening music for *Beggar's Opera* because such accompaniment used for seating purposes.

176 Lewis, Wilmarth and Philip Hofer, Compilers. *The Beggar's Opera by Hogarth and Blake.* Cambridge: Harvard University Press, 1965.

Hogarth and Blake depictions of the opera.

177 Loiseau, J. "John Gay et le *Beggar's Opera.*" *Revue Anglo-Americaine*, 12 (October 1934), 3-19.
> Satire successful because blends universal and particular.

178 McSpadden, Joseph Walker. *Light Opera and Musical Comedy*. New York: Thomas Crowell, 1946, pp. 186-188.
> Brief listing of Gay with run of opera and argument that it lampoons foreign affectations and social-political conditions.

179 Mais, Stuart Peter Brodie. "Such a Book as *The Beggar's Opera.*" *Why We Should Read —.* London: Grant Richards, 1921, pp. 58-62.
> We should read *Beggar's Opera* for the same reason we read Fielding--so very English, full of English music, robust, free from sentimentality and a "racy and true picture of human nature stripped naked" yet without savagery.

180 Mark, Jeffrey. "Ballad Opera And Its Significance in the History of English Stage Music." *The London Mercury*, 8 (July 1923), 265-278.
> Survey opera and background of *Beggar's Opera*, which prompted others (Fielding, Ralph, Cibber and Carey) to satirize foreign music. *Achilles* attacks bombastics.

* 181 Miles, William Augustus. A Letter to Sir John Fielding, Knt. Occassioned by His Extraordinary Request to Mr. Garrick for the Suppression of the *Beggar's Opera* (1773).

182 Moore, Robert Etheridge. *Hogarth's Literary Relationships*. Minneapolis: University of Minnesota Press, 1948, pp. 85-92, 103-104 and references in passing to *Beggar's Opera* and *Trivia*.
> On Hogarth's affiliation with theatre and *Beggar's Opera*.

183 Nettleton, George Henry. "The Drama and the Stage." *The Cambridge History of English Literature*. New York: Putnam's; Cambridge: University Press, 1913. X, 79.

Brief reference to *Beggar's Opera* for its introduction
of popular lyrics, political and social satire, satire
on Italian opera and anticipation of burlesques of
Fielding and Carey.

I84 ---. *English Drama of the Restoration and Eighteenth Century
(1642-1780)*. New York: Macmillan, 1928; rpt. Cooper
Square, 1968, pp. 189-194.
Standard information on satire. The play was proof
to Cibber of "vulgar taste," anticipates Fielding's
farces and has only mild portion of Swiftean *saeva
indignatio*.

I85 Nicoll. Allardyce. "The Beggar's Opera and Pantomime."
British Drama. New York: Barnes and Noble, 1963,
pp. 175-178.
Beggar's Opera invented "almost by chance, by the
erratic John Gay" whose earlier works display taste
for farce.

I86 ---. *History of Early Eighteenth Century Drama, 1700-1759*.
Cambridge: University Press, 1927, pp. 132-138, 237-
341.
Beggar's Opera catalogues as farce; *Wife of Bath*
under comedies of manners. In *Beggar's Opera*
chapter, Nicoll traces presence of song and opera's
imitators. Appendix contains documents connected
with history of stage and hand list of plays.

I87 [Handley-Taylor, Geoffrey and Frank Granville Barker.]
*Ninth Music Book, Containing John Gay and the Ballad
Opera [The Beggar's Opera]*. London: Hinrichsen, 1956.
Single volume dedicated to artifacts, plates and com-
mendatory pieces: production-oriented with producer
and critics' essays on generic features, music, satire,
cast lists, source notes, selected bibliography.
Rev. by Eric Blom in *Music and Letters*, 38 (April 1957),
195-196.

I88 Oxberry. *Anecdotes of the Stage*. London: Printed by C.
Baynes, 1827, p. 9.
"Unquestionably" a work of several hands: notes

various song contributors.

189 Pearce, Charles E. *Polly Peachum, The Story of Lavinia Fenton and The Beggar's Opera.* London: S. Paul, 1913; rpt. New York: Benjamin Blom, 1968.

> Biographical study of Lavinia Fenton with wealth of contemporary materials. Play intended to rival, not ridicule, Italian opera. Pearce includes many contemporary practices of stage, Hogarth's works on the play, background of players, moral reactions, and foibles of *Polly*. Appendix contains list of actresses who played Polly.

190 "Pinafore's Predecessor." *Harper's New Monthly Magazine*, 60 (March 1880), 501-509.

> Calls for revivals of *Beggar's Opera* and Sheridan's *Duenna*. Perhaps Richard Brome's *A Joviall Crew* suggested Gay's opera to him. Also includes popular anecdotes, popular phrases used in Bartlett's collection, and discussion of Sheridan.

191 Pope, Alexander. *The Dunciad*. Ed. James Sutherland. London: Methuen, 1943, p. 190.

> Bk. III, v. 326 has note in which Pope reports on unprecedented success of play, which was acted 63 days; actual number has been corrected to 62. Sutherland adds a note on performance and *Polly*.

192 Preston, John. "The Ironic Mode: A Comparison of *Jonathan Wild* and *The Beggar's Opera*." *Essays in Criticism*, 16 (July 1966), 268-280.

> Gay uses irony for thinking, Fielding for speaking; Fielding performs more verbal mock-heroic, while Gay's ironic effect goes beyond.

* 193 Rafroidi, Patrick. "Les fortunes d'un geux." *Faculté des Lettres de Strasbourg*, 46 (1967), 355-362.

194 Rees, John, Jr. "'A Great Man in Distress': Macheath as Hercules." *University of California Studies: Series in Language and Literature*, 10 (February 1966), 73-77.

Macheath's dilemma in III, xi resembles ancient
allegory of Hercules choosing between vice and
virtue. Gay read story in original and it was evident
in many paintings, woodcuts, essay by Shaftesbury
and in emblem books.

195 Reynolds, Myra. *"The Beggar's Opera." The Drama*, 11
(April 1921), 227-231.
Includes pictures of actors in current production,
history of production of editions, fears about moral
dangers and popularity of songs.

* 196 Rutter, Frank. "Charles Dickens and 'The Beggar's Opera.'"
Bookman (March 1922).

197 Ryan, Richard. *Dramatic Table Talk of Scenes, Situations
and Adventures Serious and Comic in Theatrical History
and Biography.* London: John Knight and Henry Lacey,
1725.
I, 25-27: Includes Swift's suggestion, Pope's recol-
lection of first night and letter about suppressing
play due to rise in thievery.
I, 75: Colman in 1780 travestied play by putting all
women in men's parts and vice versa.
I, 254-255: Gay's financial share in profits.
I, 267: Lavinia Fenton's salary raised.
I, 282: Queensberrys asked to absent selves from
court; reprints Duchess' letter of response.
II, 262-263: Account of Gay's offer of post of Gentleman Usher and fame and success of his play.
III, 206: Adam Hallam translated play but brought
it back, rather than alter it for moral purposes.

198 Sands, Mollie. "'The Beggar's Opera' Again." *The Monthly
Musical Record*, 80 (October 1950), 208-212.
Review of Pollys after Lavinia Fenton, especially
Charlotte Brent (1735) and Isabella Vincent (1760).

* 199 Sarrazin, Gregor. *John Gay's Singspiela.* Weimar, 1898.

John Gay

I100 Sawyer, Paul. "The Popularity of Various Types of Enter-
      tainment at Lincoln's Inn Fields and Covent Garden
      Theatres, 1720-1733." *Theatre Notebook*, 24 (Summer
      1970), 54-63.
          Study of ballad opera and pantomime popularity.
          Pantomime declined in 1727-1735, partly due to
          Beggar's Opera and then *Achilles*.

I101 Schultz, William Eben. *Gay's Beggar's Opera; Its Content,
      History and Influence*. New Haven: Yale University
      Press, 1923.
          Excellent study of play: includes background of first
          production, correspondence of Pope, Swift and Gay,
          plus artifacts surrounding production. Subsequent
          chapters cover original cast, continuing playing his-
          tory with changes, using wealth of evidence. Chapter
          11 begins analysis of origins and generic novelty,
          plus review of opera history. Discussion of music is
          supported by valuable appendix which describes ballad
          operas after Gay and originals for his ballads. Un-
          written influences stronger than possible specific
          sources. Schultz also reviews political and social
          satire, *Polly* and moral question.

I102 ---. "The Music of *The Beggar's Opera* in Print." *Pro-
      ceedings of the Music Teacher's National Association*,
      19th Series (1924), 87-99.
          Reviews musical background, history of published
          editions of music without literary text and includes
          extensive list with some annotations of special
          musical eds. from 1732-1921.

I103 Seldes, Gilbert. "Our Beggar's Opera." *The Dial*, 71
      (March 1921), 303-306.
          Little on *Beggar's Opera:* study of how Ziegfeld,
          Cohan and Irving Berlin learned from Gay.

I104 Sherburn, George. "A Theatre Party of 1729." *Harvard
      Library Bulletin*, 4 (Winter 1950), 111-114.
          Two letters of 5th Earl of Cork and Orrey contain
          probably imaginary story of 1729 spring theatre

party because there was no performance of *Beggar's Opera* on that night.

I105 Sherwin, Judith Johnson. " 'The World is Mean and Man Uncouth.' " *Virginia Quarterly Review*, 35 (1959), 258-270.

> Brecht ground in 20th-century disillusion, whereas Gay holds eighteenth-century faith. "Moral revulsion" abounds in Brecht's version, since the difference between the two plays is between "expose" and "denunciation." Gay displays concealed evil, whereas Brecht sees moral perversion. Thus, Brecht lacks charm of Gay and leaves audience with more somber mood.

* I106 Siegmund-Schultz, Dorothea. "Betrachtungen zur satirisch-polemischen Tendenz in John Gays *Beggar's Opera*." *Wissenschaftliche Zeitschrift der Martin-Luther Universitat Halle-Wattenberg. Geseleschafts und Sprachwissenschaft-liche Reihe*, 12 (1963), 1001-1014.

I107 Smith, Dane Farnsworth. *The Critics in the Audience of the London Theatres from Buckingham to Sheridan, A Study of Neoclassicism in the Playhouse, 1671-1779.* Alber-querque: University of New Mexico Press, 1953, pp. 45-51, 172-173. University of New Mexico Publications in Language and Literature, No. 12.

> Reviews satire of *Three Hours*, Breval's *Confederates*. *Beggar's Opera* classed as satire on Italian opera, Walpole, government satire which Fielding continued.

I108 Smith, Robert A. "The Great Man Motif in *Jonathan Wild* and *The Beggar's Opera*." *CLA Journal*, 2 (1959), 183-184.

> Ambition will destroy the great man, whether states-man or thief. Fielding used biographical prose narrative and Gay a musical to demonstrate this thesis, though punishment is milder in the opera. Thus, the two works share themes of evil, mismanagement, tyrannical rule, ambition and cruelty.

I109 Stevens, David Harrison. "Some Immediate Effects of *The*

Beggar's Opera.'' The Manly Anniversary Studies in Language and Literature. Chicago: University of Chicago Press, 1923, pp. 180-189.

Studies struggle of nobility to exercise control over theatre by examining state documents and news journals of 1728-1731 which reveal Walpole effected party journalism. *Senator* belittled opera's political satires and journals which supported Gay. Principal supporters of Gay were *The Craftsman* and *Mist's Journal.*

I110 Sutherland, James R. "The Beggar's Opera." *Times Literary Supplement,* 25 April 1935, p. 272.

Gay interested in Wild's 1725 trial. Anecdote in *Flying Post* (11 January 1728-1729) concerns underworld model for Peachum and alludes to "genuine *Peachum* (executed a few years ago)."

* I111 Swaen, A. E. H. "The Airs and Tunes of John Gay's Beggar's Opera." *Anglia,* 43 (1919), 152-190.

I112 Swift, Jonathan. *The Intelligencer.* London: A Moor, 1729, pp. 15-25.

Praises humor in *Beggar's Opera,* reviews Gay's fortunes at court, asserts religion and morality profit from Gay's placing of vice in odious light. Swift wonders why Herring condemns a play so innocent and moral; concludes only servile could object.

I113 Thorndike, Ashley H. *English Comedy.* New York: Macmillan, 1929, pp. 391-396.

Witty relief of songs controls heavy satire; Lyric stage tradition of *Beggar's Opera,* which caused imitations and revisions, runs through Gilbert and Sullivan.

I114 *The Times,* 9 March 1940, p. 4.

Reprints Burney's appraisal of Pepusch and Hawkins' partial account of his court service in Berlin; credits Pepusch as "composer" of *Beggar's Opera* rather enthusiastically.

I115 Toye, Francis. "Opera in England." *English Review*, 10
(December 1911), 115-168.
> Long essay with only scant references blaming
> *Beggar's Opera* for failure of Handel's operatic
> season. German historians call the play "direct
> ancestor of the German Singspiele," like Mozart's
> *Die Entführung alls dem Serail.*

I116 Trowbridge, Sir St. Vincent. "Making Gay Rich,and Rich
Gay." *Theatre Notebook*, 6 (October-December 1951),
14-20.
> Examines Rich's books at Lincoln's Inn Fields and
> Covent Garden for Gay's share. Corrects number of
> performances recorded in Wyndham's *Annals.*

I117 Tufts, George. "Ballad Operas: A List and Some Notes."
Musical Antiquary, 4 (January 1913), 61-86.
> 1800 entries: fills in incomplete list of ballad operas
> in Grove's *Dictionary*. Swift's famous suggestion
> prompted Gay to write *Newgate's Garland* (1725);
> Ramsay might deserve credit for prompting Gay to
> write *Beggar's Opera.*

I118 Urban, Sylvanus. "Historical Chronical." *The Gentleman's
Magazine*, (September 1773), pp. 463-464.
> Sir John Fielding protested impropriety of performing
> the play because of thievery; Garrick thought Field-
> ing's plan inconveient but promised to try for prohi-
> bition. Despite play's humor, it is "thief's creed
> and common Prayer book."

I119 Walkley, Arthur B. "Beggar's Opera." *Pastiche and Pre-
judice*. New York: A. A. Knopf, 1921, pp. 127-132.
> Play is the *H.M.S. Pinafore* of its time: analysis of
> parallels to Gilbert-Sullivan in character and moods.
> Realism and burlesque captured London with Hogarth-
> ian atmosphere on stage (Includes comments on Hammer-
> smith revival).

* I120 Walters, Eurof. "John Gay, A Devon Wit." *Taw and Torridge
Festival Programme Book* (1953).

1121 Wardle, Ralph M. "Hazlitt on *The Beggar's Opera.*" *South Atlantic Quarterly*, 70 (Spring 1971), 256-264.
Discussion of Hazlitt's remarks on Gay: performances, moral purpose and interest in low life.

1122 Weisstein, Ulrich. "Brecht's Victorian Version of Gay: Imitation and Originality in *Dreigroschenoper.*" *Comparative Literature Studies*, 7 (September 1970), 314-335.
Beggar's Opera a typical political satire whereas Brecht's play a universal one with little contemporary references. Gay parodies Handelian opera while Brecht's play is a prototype of anti-Wagnerian *Gesamtkunstwerk* with original tunes and lyrics.

1123 Westrup, J. A. "French Tunes in 'The Beggar's Opera' and 'Polly.'" *Musical Times*, 1022 (April 1928), 320-323.
French tunes in play were accessible to Gay in English sources. Westrup compares tunes 13, 19, 20 and 60 to their French sources to show Gay's English orientation. However, Gay may have consulted French sources directly for *Polly;* or, perhaps a friend supplied them.

1124 Wheatley, Henry B. *Hogarth's London, Pictures of the Manners of the Eighteenth Century.* London: Constable, 1909, pp. 305-311, 317-321 and references in passing.
Reviews background of play, Hogarth's pictures and benefit tickets, anecdotes from Baker's *Bio. Dramatica*, Angelo's *Reminiscences* and moral reactions.

1125 White, Eric W. "*Beggar's Opera* note." *Theatre Notebook*, 8 (October-December 1953), 24.
Copy of fifth edition of play has manuscript addition at end of third Act, sixth Scene with insignificant exchange between Peachum and Trapes.

1126 ---. *Rise of the English Opera.* London: Lehmann, 1951, pp. 66-68, 171-172, 198-200 and references in passing.
Reviews *Beggar's Opera* and *Polly* with focus on Britten, Dent and Austin revivals.

1127 Williams, I. A. "The Author of 'The Beggar's Opera.'"
      London Mercury, 3 (December 1920), 166-179.
          Reviews life and works, praises *Fables* and detailed
          awareness of country. *Wine* dull; *Rural Sports* first
          "remarkable" work with description, like *Shepherd's
          Week; What d'ye Call It* too general for burlesque;
          Three Hours dull. Not entirely about *Beggar's Opera*.

* 1128 Wood, F. T. "John Gay of *The Beggar's Opera*." *Bookman*,
      83 (December 1932), 162-164.

1129 Wood, Ruth Kedzie. "A Play that Has Run for Two Centuries."
      The Mentor, 15 (January 1928), 48-51.
          Sketchy study of Gay, acting history of *Beggar's
          Opera*, which set model for future comic operas, in-
          cluding Gilbert and Sullivan.

* 1130 Zweifel, Annarosa. "La *Beggar's Opera* di John Gay e la
      Dreigro Schenoper di Bertolt Brecht." *Studii e ricerchedi
      litterature inglese e americana*. Ed. Agostino Lonbardo.
      Milano: Ist. Editoriale Cisalpino, 1967.

John Gay

Productions of The Beggar's Opera

J1 Aldrich, Richard. "The Beggar's Opera." *Musical Discourse From the New York Times.* Oxford: 1928; rpt. Freeport, New York: Books for Libraries, 1967, pp. 103-125.
Review of Greenwich Village Prod. on 29 December 1920 and bowdlerizations of play. Gay hummed tunes to Pepusch. First American production on 5 December 1720 by Philadelphia company; possible one in 1732.

J2 "Another Assault by the Soviet Theater." *The Literary Digest*, 4 February 1933, p. 18.
Revival of play conforms heavily to Soviet propoganda: review contains quotes from *Manchester Guardian* report.

J3 Baring, Maurice. "The Beggar's Opera." *Punch and Judy and Other Essays.* Garden City, New York: Doubleday, Page and Co., 1924, pp. 343-348.
In review of Hammersmith prod. Baring preoccupied by general lack of such native music.

J4 Barker, John W. "Mr. John Gay's *The Beggar's Opera.*" *American Record Guide*, 29 (December 1962), 288-289, 292.
Full facsimile of Gay's text with essays by Kronenberger and Goberman reviewed: preferrable to Austin's recording, though dialogue heavily cut.

J5 ---. "The Old Vic *Beggar's Opera*, now in Stereo via Seraphim," *American Record Guide*, 34 (July 1968), 1038-1039.
Reissue of 1955: Goberman cut dialogue drastically and used separate cast of singers.

* J6   *Bath Chronicle*, 28 January 1924.

* J7   *Bath Herald*, 28 January 1924.

J8   Baxter, Beverly. *Sunday Express*, 7 June 1953.
   Review of film.

J9   "The 'Beggar' Again." *Newsweek*, 10 July 1950, p. 80.
   Bucci prod. not up to quality of 1920 Hammersmith.

J10 "The Beggar's Opera." *The Catholic World*, 171 (August 1950), 390.
   Negative review of Britten's alterations of songs.

J11 "The Beggar's Opera." *Musical Courier*, 13 January 1921, p. 56.
   Greenwich Village Theatre production.

J12 "The Beggar's Opera." *National Review*, 114 (April 1940), 414-415.
   March 5th at Haymarket.

J13 *"The Beggar's Opera."* *Theatre Arts Monthly*, 41 (May 1957), 21.
   March 13, 1957 adaptation of play by N. Y. City Center Light Opera Co.; stresses political topicality.

J14 "Beggar's Opera." *Time*, 25 December 1939, p. 46.
   Report of U.S. radio production by Goset Honti.

J15 "The Beggar's Opera at the Haymarket." *New Statesman*, 16 March 1940, p. 364.
   Gielgud production.

J16 "The Beggar's Opera at the New." *New Statesman*, 1 March 1941, p. 213.
   Sadlers' Wells production.

J17 "Beggar's Opera Produced at New Hope." *Musical Courier*, 124 (August 1941), 13.
   Pennsylvania production at Bucks County Playhouse.

John Gay

J18 Bentley, Eric Russell. "Sir Laurence Macheath." *The Dramatic Event, An American Chronicle.* New York: Horizon, 1954, pp. 140-143.
  Laurence Olivier's poor singing prompts review of his acting failures; also reviews attempts at reviving the play.

J19 Blom, Eric. "Beggar's Opera." *The Observer*, 20 April 1952, p. 6.
  Death of Austin prompts recall of Hammersmith production and work by Austin and Dent.

J20 Brereton, Austin. "The Story of 'The Beggar's Opera.'" *Graphic*, 5 June 1920, p. 910.
  Eve of Hammersmith revival prompts review of play's background.

J21 Carb., D. *Vogue*, 15 May 1928, pp. 77, 122.

J22 Compton-Rhodes, R. *"The Beggar's Opera* in Birmingham." *Times Literary Supplement*, 20 December 1923, p. 896.
  List of revivals in Birmingham: first in 1752.

J23 *Connoisseur*, 24 (August 1909), 248-249.

* J24 *Daily Telegraph*, 20 April 1929.

J25 Del Mar, Norman. "The Chamber Operas." *Benjamin Britten, A Commentary on His Works from a Group of Specialists.* Ed. Donald Mitchell and Hans Keller. London: Rockliff, 1952, pp. 163-185.
  Thorough study of adaptations Britten made of Gay's play.

J26 Dent, Alan. "Neither Good Nor Bad." *The Illustrated London News*, 27 June 1953, p. 1096.
  Film review plus Hazlitt, Boswell and Johnson opinions. Olivier's singing poor.

J27 *Design in the Theatre. Commentary by George Sheringham, James Laver, together with literature contributed by*

64

> *E. Gordon Craig, Charles B. Cochran and Nigel Playfair.*
> Ed. Geoffrey Holme. Leicester Square: The Studio, 1927.
> Contains one page of costume designs from Hammer-
> smith production.

* J28 *Doncaster Educational Committee Arts Bulletin, No. 5*
(December 1950).
British Poetry-Drama Guild production.

J29 Downes, Olin. *"Beggar's Opera* Seen at Columbia." *New
York Times*, 7 April 1954, p. 40.
Columbia University production by Bretano and
Bukofzer.

J30 *Dramatic Mirrour*, 8 January 1921, p. 59.
Hammersmith production.

J31 Evans, Powys. *The Beggar's Opera: Caricatures.* London:
Cecil Palmer, 1922.
Short review of Gay's life with caricatures of actor
from Hammersmith production.

J32 F., D. C. "The Newest Plays." *Theatre World*, 33 (April
1940), 79, 92-93 (pictures).
Austin-Gielgud production.

J33 Findon, B. W. *"The Beggar's Opera* and *Polly."* *The Play
Pictorial*, 42 (1923), 20A, 21, 25-44, 46.
Pictures of Hammersmith production with comments
on music, moral purpose and *Polly.*

J34 Fraser, Grace L. *Studio*, 19 (June 1940), 211.

J35 Gildes, Rosamond. "Rainbow Over Broadway." *Theatre
Arts*, 31 (March 1947), 16-17.
Walkins-Sheppard musical comedy with nineteenth-
century gunmen and thieves.

J36 Goossens, Eugene. "Observations on the tour of 'The Beggar's Opera.' " *The Stage*, 17 February, 25 August,
22 September, and 6 October 1921.

John Gay

J37 Graham, Lawrence. "The Beggar's Opera." *Millgate* (April 1940).

J38 "Granddaddy of the Musical: Two Hundred and Eleven Year Old 'Beggar's Opera' wins Radio Presentation." *Newsweek*, 18 December 1939, pp. 43-44.
NBC Blue Network broadcast.

* J39 Granville-Barker, Frank. "The Beggar on the Screen." *Music and Musicians* (June 1953).
Film review.

J40 *Graphic*, 29 September 1928, p. 499.
Picture of Brecht-Weill version.

J41 Green, E. Mawley. "Echoes from Broadway." *Theatre World*, 43 (March 1947), 24.
Review of *Beggar's Holiday*.

J42 *Guardian*, 15 July 1963, p. 7.

J43 H., C. "A Revised Version of 'The Beggar's Opera.'"
The Spectator, 28 January 1922, p. 113.
Austin's work in Hammersmith revival. Gay intended to rival Italian opera and was more responsible for ballad work than Pepusch.

J44 Hazlitt, William. *A View of the English Stage, or, A Series of Dramatic Criticisms.* London: Printed for Robert Stodart, 1818.
November 14, 1815 notes on success of new actors on stage.

J45 "Mister Hornblow Goes to the Play." *Theatre Magazine*, 33 (March 1921), 179-180.
Cast list and note on Greenwich Village production.

J46 Hunt, Leigh. *Leigh Hunt's Dramatic Criticism, 1808-1831.*
Ed. Lawrence H. Houtchens and Carolyn W. Houtchens. New York: Columbia University Press, 1949, pp. 75-77.

(Written 12 September 1812): praises Mrs. Sterling as Polly, Incledon as Macheath, Gay's appeal to common life, songs.

J47 Hussey, Dyneley. " 'The Beggar's Opera' Again." *Spectator,* 28 February 1941, p. 227.
New Theatre production by Sadler's Wells.

J48 ---. "Dickens Goes Gay." *Spectator,* 15 March 1940, p. 361.
Gielgud production with Dickensian quality in characters avoids being repeat of Hammersmith.

J49 Jacobson, Robert. "Sargent's Masterful 'Beggar's Opera.' " *Saturday Review,* 24 February 1968, p. 71.
Brief note on Seraphim recording by Old Vic Co.; includes review of Pepusch's role and general satire.

J50 Knight, Arthur. "Sir Laurence's Opus 3." *Saturday Review,* 15 August 1953, pp. 29-30.
Film review.

J51 Lawrence, W. J. " 'The Beggar's Opera' in Dublin." *Notes and Queries,* 13 May 1905, pp. 364-365.
First Dublin performance in middle of March 1727/8, as advertisements prove. Lawrence corrects misdating of Swift letter to Gay.

J52 Lejeune, C. A. "Gay and Glorious." *The Observer,* 7 June 1953, p. 11.
Movie review.

J53 Lewisohn, Ludwig. "The Beggar's Opera." *The Nation,* 19 January 1921, p. 91.
Reviews Greenwich Village production, Playfair revival, moral context of play and Italian opera satire.

J54 ---. "Lonely Classics." *The Drama and the Stage.* New York: Harcourt, 1922, pp. 140-144.
Brief review: includes nineteenth-century bowdlerizations and authenticity of Playfair production.

John Gay

J55 *Life*, 24 February 1947, p. 75.
Review of *Beggar's Holiday* production.

J55 Loewenberg, Alfred. "The Beggar's Opera." *Notes and Queries*, 16 (June 1945), 260.
Corrects error that Thomas Linley wrote new songs in 1777 for production; Linley wrote new orchestral accompaniments for revival at Drury Lane (8 November 1777) but they were first used in 1779 and never printed or preserved in manuscript form.

J56 Marshall, Norman. *The Other Theatre*. London: John Lehmann, 1947, pp. 33, 35-37.
Playfair altered play into "gay, neat, dainty entertainment."

* J57 Matthews, J. B. "Beggar's Opera." *Englishwoman's Domestic Magazine* (London) vol. 14, 290 and vol. 60, 501.

J58 Meltzer, Charles Henry. "Revival of 'The Beggar's Opera.'" *Theatre Magazine*, 33 (February 1921), 88, 132.
Greenwich Village production with note on original music and comparison to Gilbert.

J59 Merkling, Frank. "*The Beggar's Opera*." *Opera News*. 16 December 1961, p. 6.
Review of facsimile edition with Kronenberger and Goberman commentaries.

J60 ---. "*The Beggar's Opera*." *Opera News*. 15 December 1962, p. 36.
British recording includes 69 tunes, though stripped of much dialogue.

J61 Meyer, Annie Nathan. "Appropos of the Revival of 'The Beggar's Opera.'" *The Bookman*, 52 (February 1921), 521-524.
Greenwich Village production prompts reprint of reactions to original production, including Swift's favor, rebuke of pamphleteer, Garrick, Addison and Hawkins remarks plus preface from *What d'ye Call It*. Gay's

innovations lie in part he gave to low characters.

* J62   Myers, Denis. "The Secret of 'The Beggar's Opera.'"
        Picturegoer, 3 January 1953.
        Film review.

J63   *New Statesman*, 16 March 1935, pp. 381-382.
        Criterion Theatre revival.

J64   *Newsweek*, 6 January 1947, p. 64.
        Beggar's Holiday production.

J65   ---, 19 June 1948, p. 75.
        Britten production.

J66   "Notes of the Day: *The Beggar's Opera*." *Monthly Musical
        Record*, 70 (May 1940), 73-76.
        Prompted by recent wrangling in *Sunday Times* over
        altered songs in Gielgud revival, author calls for
        modern Gay and Pepusch to lash vice with melody.

* J67   "Observations on Scottish Presentations of 'The Beggar's
        Opera.'" *Caledonian Mercury*, 4 June 1733.

J68   *The Observer*, 21 July 1963.
        Film review.

J69   "Old *Beggar* in New Clothes." *Time*, 27 September 1948,
        p. 70.
        Review of Britten production with alterations in music.

J70   "An Opera for Schools." *Times Educational Supplement*,
        20 April 1951, p. 299.
        Announcement of Council of British Poetry-Drama
        Guild forming touring company to present new version
        of play during festival year in communities and
        schools.

* J71   "Original Beggar's Opera at Columbia University." *Musical
        America* (May 1954).

J72 "Our Grandfathers' Favorite Opera Here Again." *The Literary Digest*, 22 January 1921, pp. 28-29.
> Slight references of *Beggar's Opera:* reprints Aldrich letter in *N.Y. Times* which claims Gay hummed tunes to Pepusch, who then wrote lyrics and reprints notes on Gilbertian quality of revivals (including Greenwich Village production).

J73 Peet, Creighton. "'The Beggar's Opera.'" *Outlook and Independent*, 27 May 1931, p. 123.
> Movie barely resembles play but good: gangster and communism themes visible.

J74 Playfair, Nigel. "'The Beggar's Opera': Old Style" (Chapter 5) and "'The Beggar's Opera': New Style" (Chapter 6). *The Story of the Lyric Theatre*. London: Chatto and Windus, 1925, pp. 65-112.
> (5) Musings on intentions of original, extent of Gay's authorship, Lavinia Fenton and reactions.
> (6) Review of Hammersmith revival, Lovat Fraser's work, reactions and note by Frederic Austin on music.

* J75 "Presentation of 'The Beggar's Opera': at Lewes." *Sussex Weekly Adventurer*, 30 June 1755.

J76 Pryce Jones, David. "Crowns Away." *The Spectator*, 26 July 1963, p. 110.
> Review of Peter Wood production with Raymond Leppard arrangement of music.

J77 Ranalow, Frederic. "The Perennial Popularity of 'The Beggar's Opera.'" *Arts and Decoration*, 17 (August 1922), 297, 299.
> Ranalow was Macheath in Hammersmith production and comments on the revival.

* J78 Randall, A. W. G. *New World* (London), 3 (August 1920), 276.

J79 Ray, Cyril. *The Sunday Times* (June 1953).
> Film review.

* J80 Rendall, V. "The author of the Beggar's Opera." *Saturday Review*, 2 July 1921, p. 9.

* J81 *Review of Reviews* (London), 67 (January 1923), 67-80. (Illustrated)

  J82 Reynolds, Myra. "The Beggar's Opera." *Drama*, 11 (April 1921), 227-231.
     After Hammersmith revival: background of production with pictures, notes on appearances of play in print and on stage, morality problem, eighteenth-century bowdlerizations and relation to Italian music.

  J83 Rosenfeld, S. M. *Strolling Players and Drama in the Provinces, 1660-1765.* London: Cambridge University Press, 1939.
     Many references in passing to playing of *Beggar's Opera.*

  J84 "Round and About the Folk Songs and 'The Beggar's Opera.'" *Disc*, 5 (Autumn 1951), 55-59.
     Review of Pepusch and Britten music. See also winter 1950 issue of *Disc* for note on historical and contemporary authenticity of Britten production.

* J85 Rouveyre, Andre. "Theatre." *Mercvre de France*, 15 November 1930, pp. 149-150.
     Review of Brecht adaptation.

  J86 "Rule Britennia." *Newsweek*, 19 July 1948, p. 75.
     Britten production.

* J87 Rutland, Harold. "Gay's Newgate Pastoral." *Radio Times*, 28 (September 1951).

  J88 Smith, Cecil. "Entry of 'The Warrior' Into Valhalla." *Theatre Arts*, 31 (March 1947), 27.
     On *Beggar's Holiday.*

  J89 Strachan, Lionel R. M. "*The Beggar's Opera* in Dublin." *Notes and Queries*, 29 July 1905, p. 91.

Letter (10 May 1728) of Swift's from Dublin reports play acted twenty times to full houses; corrects previous misdating.

J90 Swinnerton, Frank. *"The Beggar's Opera."* *The Nation*, 12 June 1920, pp. 340-341.
Favorable review of Hammersmith production.

J91 Tarn. "An Odd Mixture." *Spectator*, 17 June 1922, p. 750.
Hammersmith production.

J92 ---. " 'The Beggar's Opera': One Hundredth Performance."
Spectator, 4 September 1920, pp. 304-305.
Review of Hammersmith production, Pope's comments on origin and *Dunciad* note and immediate moral controversy.

J93 *Theatre*, 8 (January 1908), 88. Drawing.
19 (March 1914), 157. Drawing.
33 (March 1921), 179. Hammersmith revival.
35 (February 1922), 77. Hammersmith revival.

J94 *Theatre Magazine*, 35 (February 1922), 77.
Scene from Hammersmith revival.

* J95 *Theatre World* (August 1925); (April 1940); (October 1948), 36-37.
Britten revival.

J96 "The Three-Penny Opera." *New Statesman*, 9 May 1931, p. 391.
Film review.

J97 *Time*, 25 December 1939, pp. 46-47.
NBC Red Network radio production.

J98 *Time*, 6 January 1947, p. 57.
On *Beggar's Holiday*.

J99   *Time*, 27 September 1948, p. 70; 13 February 1956, p. 39.

J100 *"The Times* (7 June 1920)." *Specimens of English
      Dramatic Criticism, XVII-XX Centuries.* London: Oxford,
      1945, pp. 273-275.
          Playfair's Hammersmith revival of 5 June 1920 suc-
      cessful because it preserves eighteenth-century feel-
      ing; ran 1463 performances.

* J101 Truman, H. " 'The Beggar's Opera.' " *Choir* (September
      1935).

J102 "Two Hundred Years Ago." *Notes and Queries*, 8 September
      1928, p. 164.
          Reprint from *Craftsman* (7 September 1728): New
      Theatre Comedians in Haymarket, who did *Beggar's
      Opera* at Smithfield, changing to Theatrical Booth
      at Blue-Maid Alley.

J103 "Two Hundred Years Ago." *Notes and Queries*, 24 August
      1929, p. 129.
          Excerpts from *Daily Post* (25 August 1729): one an-
      nounces performance of play.

J104 West, E. Sackville. "The Beggar's Opera." *New States-
      man*, 5 June 1948, pp. 456-457.
          Britten's production at Arts Theatre in Cambridge.

J105 White, Eric Walter. *Rise of the English Opera.* London:
      Lehmann, 1951, pp. 66-68, 171-172, 198-200 and refer-
      ences in passing.
          Focus on Dent, Austin and Britten revivals.

* J106 Woffington, Peg. "Observations on her Performance in
      'The Beggar's Opera.' " *Daily Post* (London), 4 Septem-
      ber 1732.

J107 "The World and the Theatre." *Theatre Arts*, 31 (October

1947), 9.
Beggar's Holiday production shifting to all-Black
cast.

* J108   *Yorkshire Gazette* (York), 8 December 1950 and 26 January 1951.
References in British Poetry-Drama Guild production.

* J109   "Yorkshire Presentations of 'The Beggar's Opera.'"
Craven Herald (Skipton), 2 February 1951.
British Poetry-Drama Guild production.

Polly

K1 Aitken, G. A. "'Gay's 'Polly.'' " *The Athenaeum*, 5 August
1893, pp. 202-203.
Short history of pirated editions of *Polly*.

K2 Bissell, B. H. *The American Indian in English Literature
of the Eighteenth Century.* New Haven: Yale University
Press, 1925, pp. 127-130. Yale Studies in English, No. 68.
Polly an early eighteenth century attempt to show noble
Indian in drama. Cawwawkee contrasts to "rascally"
Macheath yet light tone of whole opera prohibits ideal-
ization of savage with any real serious purpose.

* K3 Blom, Eric. "*Polly:* the sequel to *Beggar's Opera.*" *Musical
Opinion* (June 1921), 773.

K4 Burgess, C. F. "John Gay and *Polly* and a Letter to the
King." *Philological Quarterly*, 47 (October 1968), 596-
598.
Duchess of Queensberry's letter exhibits more care
than her usual correspondence; perhaps she was aided
by Gay and husband. *Polly* was convenient issue for
Queensberrys to terminate relationships with court.

K5 "The Charm of Polly." *Graphic*, 6 January 1923, p. 28.
Review of *Polly* at Kingsway.

K6   Delany, Mary Granville. *A Memoir, 1700-1788.* Compiled
       by George Paston. New York: E. P. Dutton, 1900,
       pp. 45-46 with portrait.
             Review of Duchess of Queensberry's court trouble
       on behalf of *Polly* and reprint of her reply to Vice-
       Chamberlain.

K7   Dent, Edward J. "Polly." *The Nation and The Athenaeum,*
       6 January 1923, pp. 558-560.
             Review of play's political troubles, Bax and Austin
       treatments, and comparison to Gilbert's career.

K8   Doughty, Oswald. "Foreword." *Polly: An Opera-Being
       the Second Part of the Beggar's Opera.* London: Daniel
       O'Connor, 1922, pp. vii-xxiv.
             Detailed review of *Beggar's Opera* and *Polly* back-
       grounds including letters, newspapers and friends'
       opinions. *Polly* dark and has "misanthropic de-
       spair of Swift," and lacks blasé quality of *Beggar's
       Opera.*

K9   Flood, H. "The Tunes in Gay's 'Polly.'" *Graphic,* 10
       February 1923, p. 180.
             Brief note on sources of *Polly* tunes and some on
       Beggar's Opera.

K10 Fuller, John. "Cibber, *The Rehearsal at Goatham,* and
       the Suppression of *Polly.*" *Review of English Studies,*
       n.s. 13 (February 1962), 125-134.
             Investigates Cibber's role in suppression of *Polly*
       by examining rumors, letter and works on stage.

K11 Grein, J. T. "Aspects of 1922 and Prospects of 1923."
       Illustrated London News, 6 January 1923, pp. 24-25
       (pictures), 32.
             Polly at Kingsway.

* K12 Höhne, Horst. "John Gay's *Beggar's Opera* und *Polly.*"

Zeitschrift für Anglistik und Amerikanistik, 13 (1965), 232-260 (Teil I) and 341-359 (Teil II).
Discussions of *Beggar's Opera* and *Polly*. (In German)

K13 Ould, Herman. "Old Wine in New Bottles." *The English Review*, 36 (February 1923), 142-145.
Reviews Bax production and compares *Polly* to *Beggar's Opera;* Ould confesses he has never read *Polly*.

K14 " 'Polly' A Sequel to the 'Beggar's Opera.' " *Living Age*, 30 December 1922, p. 787.
Reviews history of *Polly* revivals: 1777, 1782, 1813 and modern Bax production.

K15 " 'Polly' Goes to Court." *Literary Digest*, 4 August 1923, pp. 35-36.
Court troubles of original *Polly* and Savoy revival, with excerpt from London's *Daily Chronicle*.

K16 Sherburn, George. "The Duchess Replies to the King." *Harvard Library Bulletin*, 6 (Winter 1952), 118-121.
Universal Spectator story of Queensberry's resignation and article about Duchess' confrontations with Stanhope.

K17 Straus, Henrietta. " 'Polly' and the British National Opera." *Nation*, 28 March 1923, p. 372.
Success of *Beggar's Opera* revival prompted Bax's revival of *Polly* with twentieth-century comic opera touches.

K18 Sutherland, James B. "'Polly' Among the Pirates." *Modern Language Review*, 37 (July 1942), 291-303.
Four pirated copies of *Polly* undercut profits on Gay's quarto ed. He obtained injunction against them on 12 June 1729.

K19 Swaen, A. E. H. "The Airs and Tunes of John Gay's
 Polly." *Anglia*, 60 (1936), 403-422.
>   Catalogue (with some first stanzas) of original airs
>   with locations and characteristic lines.

K20 Tarn. "'Polly' at the Kingsway." *The Spectator*, 13 January 1923, pp. 58-59.
>   Review of alterations in Bax production and com-
>   parison to *Beggar's Opera*.

K21 *"Trivia* and *Polly* by John Gay." *Times Literary Supplement*, 27 July 1922, p. 489.
>   *Polly* reveals only flashes of Gay's old skill but
>   worth reprinting because of publishing controversy.

K22 Turner, W. J. "Polly." *The New Statesman*, 30 December
 1922, p. 406.
>   Reviews Bax revival.

K23 "Two Hundred Years Ago." *Notes and Queries*, 15 June
 1929, p. 418.
>   *Universal Spectator* and *Weekly Journal* selections
>   (14 June 1729): one announces motion and judgment
>   in Chancery Suits against booksellers who vended
>   pirated eds. of *Polly*.

K24 "Two Hundred Years Ago." *Notes and Queries*, 13 April
 1929, p. 256.
>   *Universal Spectator* and *Weekly Journal* selections
>   (12 April 1729): writs served against booksellers
>   of spurious eds. of *Polly*.

K25 Westrup, J. A. "French Tunes in 'The Beggar's Opera' and
 'Polly.'" *Musical Times*, 1022 (April 1928), 320-323.
>   Gay may have turned to French sources for tunes in
>   *Polly*; or, perhaps a friend supplied them.

K26 Whiting, George W. "'To Miss Polly Peachum.'" *Times*

Literary Supplement, 16 June 1932, p. 447.
Transcription of town pastoral, an "enthusiastic
commendation" printed with Christopher Bullock's
"Woman's Revenge: or, A Match in Newgate."

Other Dramatic Works and General Essays on Drama

L1 Ault, Norman. *New Light on Pope, With Some Additions to his Poetry Hitherto Unknown.* London: Methuen, 1949, pp. 207-221 and references in passing.
    Discusses theory that Pope wrote most of epilogue to *Captives* and Prologue to *Achilles.*

L2 Baker, David Erskine. *The Companion to the Playhouse.* London: Printed for T. Becket, 1764.
    I: Lists individual plays with little comment.
    II: Biographical review with description of *Hare with Many Friends*, background of artifacts surrounding *Beggar's Opera* and its success.

L3 Bateson, F. W. *English Comic Drama, 1700-1750.* Oxford: Clarendon, 1929; rpt. New York: Russell and Russell, 1963, pp. 78-103.
    Reviews Gay's plays with generic focus, lengthy quotes, review of Gay's treatment in eighteenth century; "genial scepticism" Gay's greatest gift.

L4 Beattie, Lester Middlesworth. *John Arbuthnot, Mathematician and Satirist.* Cambridge: Harvard University Press, 1935, pp. 229-241 and references in passing.
    Arbuthnot responsible for psychological perceptions and medical references in *Three Hours.* He, not Gay, authored pamphlet to *Most Learned Doctor W--d--d* (1723).

L5 Boas, Frederick S. *An Introduction to Eighteenth-Century Drama.* Oxford: Clarendon Press, 1953, pp. 167-190.
General review of Gay's dramatic works.

L6 Bond, Donald F. "Introduction." *Series One: Essay on Wit.* Ann Arbor: The Augustan Reprint Society, 1947, pp. 1-5.
Brief analysis of *Present State of Wit.*

L7 Bowyer, John Wilson. *The Celebrated Mrs. Centlivre.* Durham: Duke University Press, 1952, pp. 194-206.
Little on Gay, but challenges Sherburn's identifications of *Three Hours* satire.

L8 Bronson, Bertrand. "The True Proportions of Gay's *Acis and Galatea.*" *Publications of the Modern Language Association,* 80 (September 1965), 325-332.
Persuasively argues that form of *Acis and Galatea* is union of literature and music. Bronson considers stock pastoral elements, mythico-pastoral masques of Gay's contemporaries, blend of Ovidian and Theocritan techniques and Handel's work with libretto.

L9 Burnet, Alexander. *Achilles Dissected: Being a Compleat Key to the Political Characters in that New Ballad Opera, Written by the late Mr. Gay.* London: Printed for W. Mears, 1733.
Review of criticisms about satire of *Achilles:* includes letter to publisher of *Daily Courant* protesting that low satire and wit too strong for ladies. After arguing that Pope and Duckett set precedents for parody of Achilles, he concludes with parody of Pope's imitation.

L10 Clinton-Baddeley, V. C. "John Gay." *The Burlesque Tradition in the English Theatre after 1660.* London: Methuen, 1952, pp. 43-51.
What d'ye Call It represents new start in burlesque:

couplets, high sentiments put in mouths of low characters and ghosts. Baddeley concentrates on Italian opera and satire, which was obscured by success of ballad opera. *Beggar's Opera* includes not only satire on Italian opera but on low and high life and government.

L11 Fuller, John. "A New Epilogue by Pope?" *Review of English Studies*, n.s. 17 (November 1966), 409-413.
Epilogue to first edition of Gay's *Wife of Bath* written by Pope.

L12 Gagen, Jean Elisabeth. *The New Woman, Her Emergence in English Drama, 1600-1730.* New York: Twayne, 1954, pp. 78-81.
Negligible references: *Three Hours* blatant farce on female wits and is mostly Gay's work.

L13 Goldstein, Malcolm. *Pope and the Augustan Stage.* Stanford: Stanford University Press, 1958, pp. 17-23, 87-88.
Analysis of satire and authorship of *What d'ye Call It* and *Three Hours*, with review of Parker's key and Breval's *Confederates*.

L14 Gray, Charles. *Theatrical Criticism in London to 1795.* New York: Columbia University Press, 1931, pp. 70, 81, 240, 274-275, 283 and references in passing.
Study of journals with theatrical criticism of *Achilles* and morality of *Beggar's Opera*.

* L15 Harrison, Elizabeth. *A Letter to John Gay on The Captives.* 1724.

L16 Hazlitt, William. "Lecture VIII. On the Comic Writers of the Last Century." *Lectures on the English Comic Writers, Delivered At the Surry Institution.* Philadelphia: Published for M. Carey and Son, 1819, pp. 302-349.

>   *What d'ye Call It* not one of Gay's "happiest things"
>   and *Polly* "complete failure."

L17 Hughes, Leo. *A Century of English Farce*. Princeton:
   Princeton University Press, 1956, pp. 90, 121-123, 249-
   252 and references in passing.
   Beggar's Opera helped ballad opera rival pantomime.
   Mohocks approaches farce with bits of true burlesque.
   What d'ye Call It closest to burlesque in tradition of
   Rehearsal. *Three Hours* (half farce, half burlesque),
   Rehearsal at Goatham contains elements; only *What
   d'ye Call It* has merit as afterpiece.

L18 Kerby-Miller, Charles. "Preface." *Memoirs of the Extraordinary life, works, and discoveries of Martinus Scriblerus. Written in collaboration by the members of the
   Scriblerus Club: John Arbuthnot, Alexander Pope, Jonathan Swift, John Gay, Thomas Parnell and Robert Har-
   ley, Earl of Oxford.* New Haven: Published for Wellesley
   College by Yale University Press, 1950, pp. 1-77.
   Contains several paragraph-length references to Gay's
   role in Scriblerus Club: portrayed as Pope's man, not
   always the most active collaborator. Gay needed
   money, so he is listed as author of *What d'ye Call It.*

L19 *A Key to the New Comedy; Call'd Three Hours After Mar-
   riage. Written by a Person of Distinction in London, To
   his Friend in the Country of Cornwal. With a Letter,
   giving an Account of the Origin of the Quarrel between
   Cibber, Pope, and Gay.* Dublin: W. Whitestone, 1957.
   More literary examination of play than Parker's
   Key.
   Available in Morton and Peterson edition of play in
   Appendix, pp. 101-111.

L20 Lewis, Peter E. "Another Look at John Gay's *The Mohocks.*"
   Modern Language Review, 63 (October 1968), 790-793.
   Mohocks burlesques Dennis' *Appius and Virginia*

(1709), as well as *Paradise Lost* and contemporary
tragic style.

L21 ---. "Gay's Burlesque Method in *The What d'ye Call It*."
Durham University Journal, 29 (1967), 13-25.
Play balance between tragedy and farce with low
world where Buckingham used courtly in *Rehearsal*.
Direct parody subordinated to overall design.

L22 Loftis, John D. "Displacement of the Restoration Tradition,
1728-1737." *Comedy and Society from Congreve to Fielding*. Stanford: Stanford University Press, 1959, pp. 101-
111.
Opposition satire in *Polly* attacks urban corruption
with primitive innocence of Indians. Detached beg-
gars in *Beggar's Opera* serve literary function like
eighteenth-century imaginary travellers.

L23 ---. *Politics of Drama in Augustan England*. Oxford:
Clarendon Press, 1963, pp. 11-12, 88-98 and references
in passing.
Review of *Three Hours* and *Captives*, *Achilles*,
opposition to Walpole in *Beggar's Opera* and
Polly's suppression.

L24 ---. *Steele at Drury Lane*. Berkeley: University of California
Press, 1952, pp. 71-73.
Steele would have prevented *What d'ye Call It* if in
town because it satirizes works he praised. *Three
Hours* touched off review of Drury Lane's short-
comings because Pope implied Steele was prominent
in opposition to play.

L25 Marks, Jeanette. *English Pastoral Drama*. London: Methuen,
1908, pp. 79-84 and references in passing.
Dione not a true pastoral because of humorous bent.
Acis and G. adds operatic to pastoral. Marks features
bibliography of English pastoral plays from 1660-1798.

L26 Morton, Richard and William M. Peterson. "Introduction."
Three Hours After Marriage by John Gay, Alexander Pope,

John Arbuthnot with The Confederates and the Two Keys.
Painesville, Ohio: Lake Erie College Studies, 1961.
I, i-xvi.
Review of play's background and attacks and keys,
plus satiric identifications. Gay, as dramatist in
group, must have controlled play.

L27 Parker, E. *A Complete Key to the New Farce, call'd Three
Hours After Marriage, With an Account of the Authors.*
London: Printed and Sold by E. Berrington, 1717.
Identifications (some disputed) and parallels to
Scriblerus writings.
Available in Morton and Peterson ed. of play in
Appendix, pp. 70-77.

L28 Sherburn, George. "The Fortunes and Misfortunes of *Three
Hours After Marriage.*" *Modern Philology,* 24 (August
1926), 91-109.
Analysis of pamphlet attacks on play and its failure;
includes satiric identifications.

L29 Smith, Dane Farnsworth. *Plays About the Theatre in England, from the Rehearsal in 1671 to the Licensing Act
in 1737 or, The Self-Conscious Stage and Its Burlesque
and Satirical Reflections in the Age of Criticism.* London: Oxford University Press, 1936, pp. 90-104, 199-
201, 136-162 and references in passing.
Analysis of rehearsal genre and imitations of *Beggar's Opera,* plus list of Gay's plays. *What d'ye
Call It* a burlesque of play forms, the first play since
"Rehearsal" to indulge in extensive parody of popular drama.

L30 ---. *The Critics in the Audience of the London Theatres
from Buckingham to Sheridan, A Study of Neoclassicism
in the Playhouse, 1671-1779.* Alberquerque: University
of New Mexico, 1953, pp. 45-51, 172-173. University of
New Mexico Publications in Language and Literature,
No. 12.
Reviews satire of *Three Hours,* Breval's *Confederates;*
classes *Beggar's Opera* as satire on Italian opera,

Walpole and government satire which Fielding continued.

L31 Smith, John Harrington. "Introduction." *Three Hours After Marriage*. Los Angeles: Clark Memorial Library of University of California, 1961, pp. 1-8. Augustan Reprint Society Nos. 91-92.
Greater part of play by Pope and Arbuthnot, who knew of potential hostility; comic caricatures strong.

L32 Stroup, Thomas B. "Gay's *Mohocks* and Milton." *Journal of English and Germanic Philology*, 46 (April 1947), 164-167.
Parallels opening scene of *Mohocks* to opening lines of "diabolical conclave" in *Paradise Lost*, vi: activities and oaths similar and poem written during period of great interest in Milton.

L33 Theobald, Lewis and Benjamin Griffin. *A Complete Key to the Last New Farce The What d'ye Call It*. London: Printed for James Roberts, 1715.
Preface dismisses farce as mere banter and jest. Key identifies significant ridicules of Shakespeare, Dryden, Philips, Southern, Rowe and Otway parodies.

L34 "Two Hundred Years Ago." *Notes and Queries*, 21 December 1929, p. 434.
Universal Spectator and *Weekly Journal* selections (21 December 1729): Gay's *Wife of Bath* in rehearsal at Theatre Royal in Lincoln's Inn Fields.

Dissertations and Theses

M1 Armens, Sven M. "John Gay as Pastoral Poet, A Study of His Views on Social Responsibility." Ph.D., Harvard University, 1951.

M2 Beckwith, Charles Emilia. "John Gay's Eclogues and Georgics. A Critical Edition (Vs. I and II)." Ph.D., Yale University, 1956. [See *Dissertation Abstracts*, 27 (1961), 4215-A].

Critical edition of works representing theme of pastoral, with collated texts, notes, appendix with "early version" of one poem and "unauthorized printing" of another; includes textual, bibliographical notes, historical and critical and biographical notes.

M3 Burgess, Chester Francis. "John Gay's 'Happy Vein' " The Ambivalent Point of View." Ph.D., Nortre Dame, 1962. [See *Dissertation Abstracts*, 23 (October-December 1962), 1348].

M4 Coleman, Mark Carney. "John Gay and the Mock-Form." Ph.D., Cornell, 1970.

M5 Cox, Mary Elizabeth. "Realism and Convention: A Study of the Poetry of Prior, Swift, and Gay." Ph.D., Ohio State, 1960. [See *Dissertation Abstracts*, 21 (February-April 1961), 2272].

Realism based on details; best poems of Prior, Swift and Gay mix correctness and restraint with realism of detail.

M6   Donahue, Sister Rita M. "The Correspondence of John Gay and Henrietta Howard, Countess of Suffolk, A Critical Edition." Ph.D., Fordham University, 1956.

M7   Goulet, Robert Gerard. "The Dramatic Art of John Gay." Ph.D., Brown University, 1969.

M8   Graham, Albert Edwin. "John Gay's *Fables*, Edited with an Introduction on the Fable as an Eighteenth-Century Literary Genre." Ph.D., Princeton, 1960. [See *Dissertation Abstracts*, 21 (February-April 1961), 2273].
Edition compares first three eds. in First Series with explanation. Introductory essay traces fable as genre until Gay's death and considers literary and biographical background to Gay's writing of his *Fables*.

M9   Hamilton, Edward M. "The Life of John Gay." Ph.D., Minnesota, 1940. Reviewed in *Summaries of Ph.D. Theses*, University of Minnesota, III, 112-115.

M10 Harris, Harold Joel. "Neo-Classical Satire: The Conservative Muse." Ph.D., Ohio State University, 1954.
Contains frequent citations of *Beggar's Opera*.

M11 Harris, Robert Brice. "The Beast in English Satire from Spencer to John Gay." Ph.D., Harvard University, 1930.

M12 Heuston, Edward Francis. "Satiric Method in John Gay's Eclogues and Georgics." Ph.D., Wisconsin, 1965.
[See *Dissertation Abstracts*, 25 (May-June 1965), 7243-4].
Gay's pastorals not merely descriptive but complex satiric pieces requiring reader's awareness of kinds of poetry imitated.

M13 Höhne, Horst. "John Gay's Bühnenwerke in Ihrem Verhaltnis zun Zeitzenossischen Dramenschaffen." Ph.D., Berlin-Humboldt, 1960.

M14 Irving, William. "John Gay's London, Illustrated from the Poetry of the Time." Ph.D., Harvard University, 1926.

An Annotated Checklist

M15 Joseloff, Samuel Hart. "John Gay and the Eighteenth-
Century Pastoral Tradition." Ph.D., Princeton, 1968.
[See *Dissertation Abstracts*, 29 (January-March 1969),
2677A].
Discussion of Gay's pastoral in relation to Augustan
concepts of eclogue and progress of Gay's career:
includes analysis of *Shepherd's Week*, town eclogues,
"other experimental eclogues," bucolic songs and
ballads and pastoral drama.

M16 Kenffel, Kenneth William. "The 'Great Man' in English
Satire, 1710-1743." Ph.D., University of Pennsylvania,
1959.
Includes *Beggar's Opera*.

M17 Klein, Julie Beth. "John Gay: The Imitative and the Unique."
Ph.D., University of Oregon, 1971.
Study of Gay's use of sources in *Shepherd's Week*,
Trivia, and *Beggar's Opera*.

M18 Lilly, Marie Loretto. "The Georgic, A Contribution to the
Study of the Vergilian Type of Didactic Poetry." Ph.D.,
Johns Hopkins, 1916.

M19 Macey, Samuel Lawson. "Theatrical Satire As a Reflection
of Changing Tastes." Ph.D., University of Washington,
1966. [See *Dissertation Abstracts*, 27 (January-March
1966), 3014].
Broad study of plays which ridicule own medium:
includes works by Gay.

M20 Nash, James F. "John Gay and the Georgic Tradition."
Ph.D., University of Virginia, 1971.

M21 Noble, Yvonne. "John Gay, *The Beggar's Opera*: A Critical
Edition." Ph.D., Yale University, 1966. [See *Dissertation Abstracts*, 27 (January-March 1967), 2539-A].
Text with dialogue and music plus critical essay
which considers contemporary atmosphere; also re-
publishes sources of airs with words and music and
airs and sources of *Polly*.

M22 Oster, Harry. "A Study of the Songs of Thomas D'Urfey,
     John Gay, Charles Dibdin, and Thomas Moore." Ph.D.,
     Cornell University, 1953.

M23 Parlakian, Nishan. "The Image of Sir Robert Walpole in
     English Drama, 1728-1742." Ph.D., Columbia University
     1967.
     More than fifty plays of period incorporate image of
     Walpole: special focus on *Beggar's Opera.*

M24 Schultz, William H. "The Beggar's Opera, By John Gay.
     Edited with a Historical and Critical Introduction and
     Notes." Ph.D., Yale University, 1915.

M25 Sessoms, Henry Morris. "The Art of Scriblerian Prose
     Satire." Ph.D., Vanderbilt, 1968. [See *Dissertation
     Abstracts*, 29 (January-March 1969), 2282A].
     Studies major collaborative works of Scriblerus Club
     to distinguish joint techniques.

M26 Shea, John Stephen. "Studies in the Verse Fable From La
     Fontaine to Gay." Ph.D., Minnesota, 1967. [See *Dis-
     sertation Abstracts*, 28 (April-June 1968), 5029A].
     Examines genre's treatment by LaFontaine, Ogilby,
     Dennis, Mandeville, and Gay plus Dryden and Mande-
     ville poems.

M27 Sherman, Dorothy Louise. "Ambivalence in the Theatre Plays
     of John Gay." Ph.D., Stanford University, 1969. [See
     Dissertation Abstracts, 30 January-February 1970) 3575-A].

M28 Sorenson, Rexford Scott. "Poet of Design: The Craftsman-
     ship of John Gay." Ph.D., Ball State University, 1970.

M29 Thompson, Keith Maybin. "Honest John Gay, A Re-estimate
     of the Man and His Work." Ph.D., New York University,
     1961. [See *Dissertation Abstracts*, 23 (July-September
     1962), 636].
     Considers Gay's relationship to British "Romantic
     tradition rather than neo-classical." Gay's satiric
     method related to medieval European tradition rather

than classical or neo-classical.

M30 Tolksdorf, Caecilie. "John Gay's Beggar's Opera Und
   Bert Brecht's Dreigroschenoper." Ph.D., Bonn, 1934.

M31 Wray, William R. "The English Fable, 1650-1800." Ph.D.,
   Yale University, 1950. [See *Dissertation Abstracts*,
   29 (July-September 1968), 619A].
   Treats traditional fable: Gay best of English
   fabulists.

Masters Theses

M32 Lowenstein, Irma. "*The Beggar's Opera* by John Gay."
   M.A., Yale University, 1950.

M33 Ryniker, Harriet E. "The Early Literary Career of John Gay."
   M.A., University of Illinois, 1941.

M34 VanArdsdale, Ronald Albert. "A Producing Director's Study
   of John Gay's *Beggar's Opera*." M.A., State University
   of Iowa, 1940.

M35 Williams, E. E. "A Critical Study of the Works of John Gay,
   with Special Reference to Invention and Craftsmanship."
   M.A., Westfield College, London University, 1959-1960.

M36 Winters, Earl Wm. "*The Beggar's Opera:* A New Production
   Script." M.A., Denver University, 1947.

M37 Wright, Harriett Cleveland. "The Development of a Costuming
   Project for a University." M.A., University of Wisconsin,
   1941.

M38 Zimmerman, S. "The Influence of Francois Villon, John Gay
   and Rudyard Kipling on the Songs in Brecht's Dreigroschenoper." M.A., Indiana University.

AUTHOR INDEX

Aden, John M. D1

Agate, James I1

Aitken, George A. C1, H1, H2, K1

Aldrich, Richard J1

Andrews, Hilda J. I2

Angelo, Henry I3

Armens, Sven M. C2, C17, M1

Arthos, John D2

Ault, Norman H3, L1

Baker, David I4, L2

Ball, F. Elrington H4, H5

Baller, Joseph H6

Banerjie, Santi Ranjan I5

Baring, Maurice I6, J3

Baring-Gould, Sabine C3

Barker, John W. J4, J5

Barnett, George L. H7

Bateson, F. W. L3

Battestin, Martin E1

Baxter, Beverly J8

Beattie, Lester M. H8, L4

Beckwith, Charles Emilia M2

Bentley, Eric R. J18

Berger, A. V. I7

Birrell, Augustine C5

Bissell, B. H. K2

Blackwell, Alfred E. A3

Blom, Eric I8, Rev. of I87, J19, K3

Boas, Frederick S. L5

Bogorad, Samuel N. F1

Bond, Donald F. Rev. of C2, L6

Bond, Richmond P. E2

Boswell, James I9

Bowyer, John Wilson L7

Brawner, J. P. Rev. of C2

Brereton, Austin J20

Brie, Frederick H9

Brockway, Wallace I11

Bronson, Bertrand I12, L8

Brown, Wallace Cable C6

Bryce, John D. G2

Brydges, E. T. I13

Burd, Henry A. E3

Burdett, Osbert C7

Burgess, C. F. B1, B2, B3, E4, F2, H10, H11, I14, I15, K4, M3

Burnet, Alexander L9

Burney, Charles I16

Bushnell, Margaret I17

Butt, John Rev. of A11, H12

C., F. W. C8

Cahoon, Herbert. Rev. of C2